Target Pistol Shooting

Target Pistol Shooting

Eliminating the Variables

P. C. FREEMAN

FABER AND FABER
London Boston

First published in 1981
by Faber and Faber Limited
3 Queen Square London WC1N 3AU
Printed in Great Britain by
Lowe and Brydone Printers Limited
Thetford, Norfolk

British Library Cataloguing in Publication Data

Freeman, Peter Cuthbert
Target pistol shooting.
1. Pistol shooting – Handbooks, manuals, etc.
I. Title
799.3'12 GV1175

ISBN 0–571–11662–0

Contents

Illustrations

Figures

Plates

Introduction

The subtitle of this book explains its purpose. Eliminating the variables requires a constant examination of technique to eliminate anything which gives rise to variation from shot to shot. An established reliable technique is the only foundation for good shooting. I hope to show that there are four principal ingredients involved which dovetail with each other to produce the overall technique. They are stance, grip, trigger release and aim. There will always be discussion about which element should be emphasized most, but, as each forms part of the whole, it is the integration that is important.

Pistol shooting, indeed all target shooting, is now a sport in its own right, no longer an adjunct of the military art. One accepts that it is potentially dangerous and must be carried out with proper safeguards. It is because of this that shooters are responsible people well aware that safety is of paramount importance. I do not propose to discuss safety in detail as this will be the first lesson for the novice and an essential element at all times in the conduct of shooting. Safety on the range, safety at home, security of arms and ammunition will become a self-imposed discipline. Incidents involving the careless handling of weapons are very rare and are always the responsibility of an individual for, in my opinion, there is no such thing as an 'accident' involving firearms.

The emphasis in this book may appear to be on deliberate or 'slow fire' shooting as distinct from timed shooting, but the basic techniques are common to each pistol discipline whether deliberate, rapid fire, timed fire, air pistol, small-bore or centrefire. Except in some specialized pistol shooting outside the realms of normal target shooting (and therefore of this book) it is always necessary to stand unsupported, hold the pistol at arm's length also unsupported, aim and fire. This book will not discuss in detail the specialized techniques required for the differing pistol disciplines. These can be acquired as the shooter's skill improves and specialization so dictates.

There is on-going examination of advances in technique, and periodically articles appear about aspects of physical and psychological matters appertaining to this developing sport. However, first the basics have to be learned and I hope that this book will both assist the novice to that end and remind the expert that his success is based on sound principles.

Pistol shooting is a sport for all ages and all the family. By classification shooters compete at their own level and can take part in open competition without being in awe of the top shooters. It is a sport to be enjoyed, although the results obtained will depend on the effort put in, and certainly one does not have to be an expert to experience the friendship that this sport engenders.

I would like to acknowledge the invaluable help that my wife, Peggy, has given me in the preparation of this book, not only in the editing but in the material itself. Until recently, as National Pistol Coaches, we had the privilege of coaching our Junior National Pistol Squad and learned much from answering their searching questions. I would also like to thank my nephew, Tony Hazell, for photographing 'Taking the Grip'.

1. Stance

The rules for normal pistol shooting stipulate that the shooter must stand unaided and hold the pistol in one hand at arm's length without artificial aids. The body must therefore be capable of adopting a sufficiently stable position to hold the pistol to produce within the required parameter a top score.

I do not propose to enter into a detailed description of the body as most shooters will have some idea of their anatomy, and the subject could fill many volumes. Suffice to say that the body consists of a skeleton with movable joints, held together and manipulated with muscles and tendons, fed through digestive, respiratory and circulatory systems and operated by a nervous system programmed through the brain either automatically or consciously.

The body must acquire the most stable position it can if the shooter is going to function efficiently. The considerations involved are the environment, the weight of the pistol, the need to exercise as precise a control as possible over the pistol, and the fitness of the shooter. The questions of grip, aim, trigger release and fitness will be dealt with in later chapters, but all involve co-ordination and muscular control.

The first aspect to be considered is the contact between the body and the ground, assuming that the body is upright. Firing platforms are generally flat and firm, but there is the occasional outdoor range where the shooter has to stand on natural ground. In such cases it is necessary to find a flat area within the allotted firing position on which to place the feet. However, it is assumed that the firing point is usually flat and level.

The link between the body and the ground is through footwear. The shooter must be consistent in his footwear. There are comfortable specialized shooting boots which give the proper support and angles between feet and ankles. If it is not possible to get shooting boots then find a suitable alternative. Boots are better than shoes, as they give support to the ankle; they should be worn with a comfortable sock. They should have flexible uppers and a sole that provides full contact between the feet and the ground. Ankle-supporting boots are desirable because when the feet are on the ground in the shooting position the thrust from the weight of the body is not only downwards but also outwards, since the feet are apart and not directly under the centre of gravity of the body (see fig. 1). The thrust against the outside of the foot is therefore contained within the ankle support. If ordinary shoes are worn, the foot will have a tendency to turn outwards and instead of the weight being over the whole of the foot it will be towards the edges, causing unnecessary strain.

The precise position of the feet in relation to the line of fire will vary from person to person, but their position in relation to the body will alter very little. The most stable support

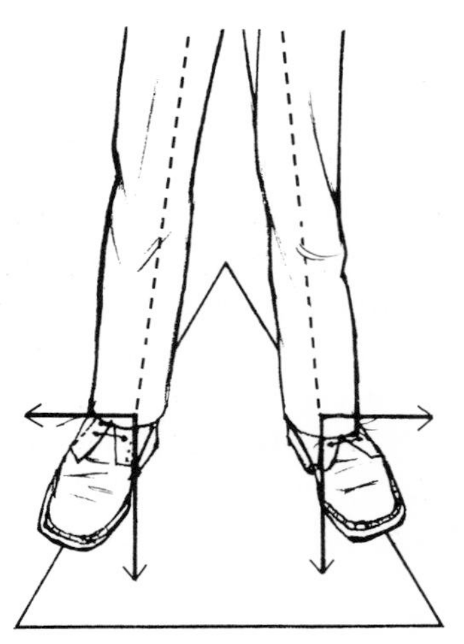

Fig. 1. *Stance*

would be a tripod as this can be adapted to suit most ground configurations. Unfortunately we have to rely on only two legs and therefore have to position the feet along two sides of a triangle to get a comparable position. The best position is along the sides of an equilateral triangle which lies within the width of the shooter's shoulders. The heels should be about twelve inches apart at an angle of 60° (see fig. 2). Individual modifications to this will depend on the shooter's physique and the actual course of fire. (Some shooters take a wider stance in rapid and centre fire.)

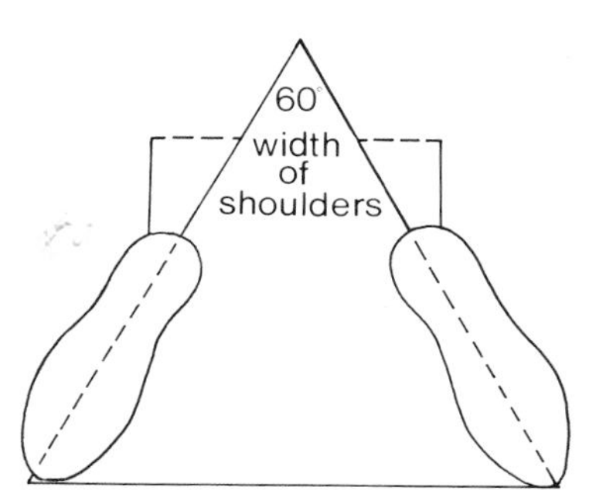

Fig. 2. *Stance: plan of feet*

Such a position will enable the body to be held erect. The centre of gravity of the body will be above the centre of the triangle and there will be no necessity for the shooter to lean forward or backwards to maintain his position. (For the moment the weight of the pistol in the outstretched arm will be disregarded.) The relationship of this triangle to the line of fire will also be considered when dealing with the raising of the pistol to the aiming position (see Chapter 4).

Now that the feet are in the correct position the rest of the body, which should be upright, can be considered. The purpose of the erect posture is to hold the head in such a position that the eyes can be used most effectively, looking straight ahead and parallel to the ground. The head can then be turned in any direction without strain and without losing the best 'seeing' position. In an asymmetrical aspect strain is imposed and the purpose of the best stance is to eliminate this. Strain imposes a handicap which detracts from the considerable effort required to produce the best result.

The shooter is now standing correctly, with the trunk held erect, looking in a level direction from the upright head. There should be no apparent strain in holding this position, the body should be relaxed and the weight of the trunk held by the pelvis. The shooter will learn to 'sit' on his hips at the same time keeping his body upright. If the body is too tense 'sway' will develop. The direction of the sway will be that in which the trunk is facing. It will not always be immediately apparent to the shooter as he will try to compensate by straining to maintain his aim. Sway will also occur if the feet are too close or too far apart. The shooter will, after a time, learn to recognize the feeling of sway and take the appropriate remedy, that is, to relax or adjust his position. It is interesting to ingredients involved which dovetail with each other to produce the overall technique. They are stance, grip, trigger

Having placed the body in the right position it is necessary to point it in the right direction. This involves picking up the pistol and taking an aim, which subjects the body to another force. It will be apparent that holding a weight of about two pounds at the extremity of the arm will tend to pull the arm down. There are two ways to overcome this and in practice both are used. Without the pistol the centre of gravity of the body will be directly above the triangle assumed by the feet, and it is desirable that this does not move too much (see fig. 3). The body will lean very slightly back to counteract the weight but not enough to disturb the position of the head which must be kept erect. The muscles of the arm and shoulder and down across the back will be brought into play to support the arm.

The arm holding the pistol must be completely unsupported, and even a watch worn on that wrist will be frowned upon. It is not worth taking any risks (and a watch is so easy to take off). The free arm should not be left in limbo, hanging at the side or it may be distracting. It should be used to support

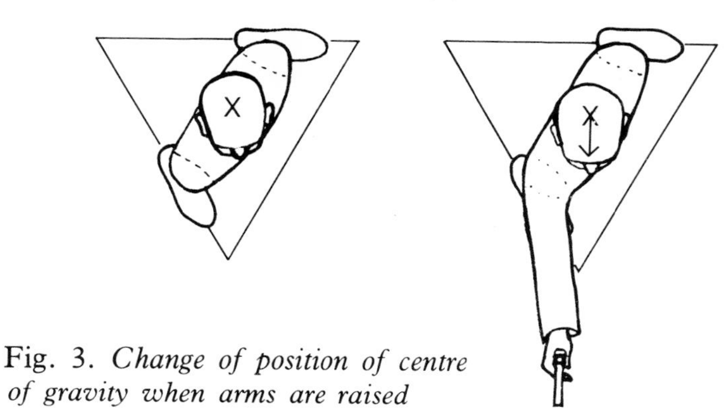

Fig. 3. *Change of position of centre of gravity when arms are raised*

the body by anchoring to the hip area. This can mean putting it into a pocket, hooking it to a belt or thrusting it into the pocket of the shooting jacket which should have been designed for that purpose. Even then it is a good idea to have something in the pocket for the hand to grasp, such as a handkerchief.

The degree to which these factors interact depends on the actual weight of the pistol and the characteristics of the individual. The arm should be extended in a natural way until it locks. For some people this will happen when the elbow is still slightly bent and with others there will be an overextension of the elbow joint. This feature will be important when building a perfect grip as it decides the angle of the wrist. The pistol has to be brought up to the line of sight so that the head remains upright. The amount the arm has to be raised will depend on the degree to which it is straightened. If the arm is slightly bent then the wrist has to be cocked more than if there is an overextension. The wrist is one of the more vulnerable joints as it carries much of the weight of the pistol.

It should be pointed out that young shooters are at risk if they maintain this stance for too long a period. It has been shown that back troubles can develop in this way, especially if exaggerated stances are taken. Any sign of back trouble should be reported and in some extreme cases it may be desirable to take up another sport to avoid permanent disability. (This fact also applies to rifle shooting.)

It is not necessary to have a detailed knowledge of the aim to align oneself on the target. It is sufficient to point the pistol at the vertical axis of the target. The following description relates to a right-handed shooter. If the left foot is parallel with the firing line an 'oblique' position is being adopted, and if the side of the triangle opposite the feet is pointing at the target an 'in-line' position is being used (see fig. 4). Each shooter will have a comfortable position somewhere between the two

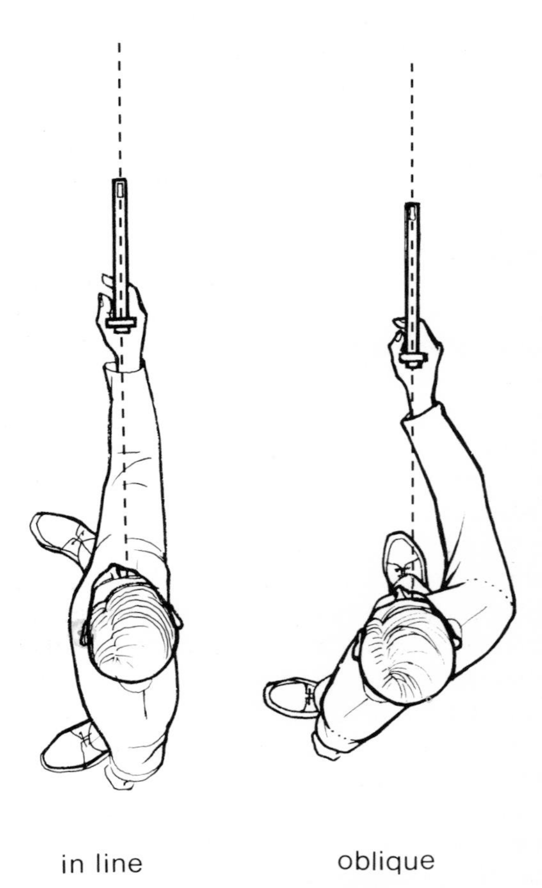

Fig. 4. *Stance: in line and oblique*

extremes and this will become his natural stance. There will be some shooters who go beyond the in-line stance.

It cannot be assumed that each shooter will adopt exactly the same stance every time. The individual must take up his natural stance each time he takes up his firing position. Standing ready to fire on the firing point he will adopt an approximate position which generally suits him. He then looks at the target, shuts his eyes and raises the pistol to the aiming position. Taking a quick look along the sights he can see whether the pistol is pointing at the vertical axis or to the left or right. If to one side or the other he will adjust the position of the feet to bring him into line. If, for instance, the pistol is pointing to the right he will move the left foot slightly to the left, adjust the right foot and then take another trial aim. This will be repeated until the shooter is quite sure that he is taking his natural aim. Occasional differences will probably depend on what physical exercise has been taken and the looseness of the shoulder joint. Some movement should be left in this joint as it is not wise to have the arm locked against the shoulder or strain will ensue. Taking the natural aim will reduce the strain because, if the aim is not central, the arm will naturally want to take up a position of equilibrium. The natural aim should be checked frequently during the shoot, especially if for any reason the feet are moved. Some shooters, having checked their stance, mark the position of the feet with a piece of chalk in case they need to leave the firing point. When the position is readopted it should be checked before firing the next shot. The natural aim can change due to tenseness in arm and back muscles at the beginning of the shoot and their subsequent relaxation during the programme. It is a simple exercise to check the position, and failure to do so could deprive the shooter of a few valuable points in an otherwise good shoot.

As previously stated, the object of the stance is to provide a stable shooting platform, but it must be emphasized that it cannot provide a perfectly still one. The body is in perpetual movement: the heartbeat pulses through it and its natural functions cannot stop for a moment. When trying to keep the pistol as motionless as possible muscles are adjusting themselves very rapidly to maintain the still position. To begin with, these movements will be seen as the pistol wobbles over the target but, as the systems get trained, the adjustments will become finer and the groups will get smaller. The skill of the shooter will largely depend on his ability to train his body to make as little movement as possible.

This is a suitable place to discuss clothing as it does have a bearing on stance. Clothing should be suited to the environment, so there can be no consistently recommended outfit, and it must never be suffered but, rather, used as a beneficial accessory. The shooter will normally be on an enclosed range and should dress for forseeable situations. If the day is cold then it is important to start and to remain warm, as it is impossible to produce a good score when cold. Warm clothing should not be restrictive and must allow easy arm movement. Lightweight woollens are preferable, even including 'long-johns', and together with a leather shooting jacket should be adequate. The heavier the garments the more weight the arm has to lift and the greater the overall expenditure of energy. When it is cold, energy must be conserved as far as possible. In hot weather as little clothing as may be desired can be worn, but it is preferable to keep reasonably covered as the effect of slight draughts on the body can be disconcerting. Whether hot or cold any changes of clothing may involve change of stance and this must be checked. (General shooting accessories will be dealt with in another chapter.)

In conclusion, the meticulous attention to detail that should be given to stance will be carried through to the other basic principles. A good stance will feel 'right' to the shooter and give him confidence. By eliminating any factors that could cause strain the shooter will be able to concentrate on the application of the other principles during his shoot.

2. Grip

The word 'grip' can cause confusion, as in this context it has two meanings. The part of the pistol that is held by the hand is the 'grip' of the pistol and the hand's action in holding the pistol is also known as the 'grip'. Both aspects will be dealt with in this chapter.

The pistol needs to be fitted to the hand and this will require alterations to the grip or stock. This part of the pistol is usually in two halves, each side being clamped to the frame. The grip will be set at an angle to the line of the pistol and this angle determines the rake of the grip. A manufacturer can only supply an average grip with his pistol, although much research will have been done at the design stage to make the rake suitable for typical customers of that pistol. When choosing a pistol, an important factor to consider is, therefore, the rake. As explained in the previous chapter, the pistol will be held with the elbow locked. The degree of extension of the elbow will determine the natural cocking of the wrist to bring the pistol into the line of sight. The greater the degree of extension, i.e. the straighter the arm, the less the wrist has to be cocked and the greater the rake needed to bring the pistol into the line of sight.

It is important, therefore, when choosing a pistol to see that the rake of the grip is nearly correct for your aim. Many different makes and types of pistol should be handled and fired before deciding on the most suitable one. Your first pistol should be as versatile as possible, i.e. it should be an auto-loading pistol capable of shooting as many different courses of fire as are in the programme. The shooter will find which course of fire is most satisfying and can then invest in a more specialized pistol for that event.

I have mentioned the 'auto-loading' pistol. I prefer this description of the magazine pistol as opposed to the single-shot pistol, as all this pistol does is to reload one shot into the chamber each time the pistol is fired. ('Semi-automatic' is another misnomer.) The single-shot pistol is now mainly a specialist pistol for the free pistol course although many others will be used for normal precision fire. The air pistol is also a single-shot pistol.

Having decided upon the most suitable pistol it will then usually be necessary for the pistol to be fitted to the shooter. Unless the shooter is experienced there should be no hurry to make any alterations. No harm will be done by using factory grips while the basic principles are learned and it may be six months before any alterations are made. Any good shooter can pick up a pistol and make a reasonable score, because with a strange weapon he will concentrate much more on the principles. Another reason for not altering grips too soon is that after a time the shooter may decide that the pistol is not suitable and may wish to exchange it for another. Its value will be greatly reduced if the grips are unsuitable for the new owner.

Any adjustment to a grip will take time as it is seldom that the right fit is achieved at once. Wooden grips are preferable to plastic as they feel better in the hand. If the fitted grips are unsuitable for alteration and if the shooter does not think he is capable of working from new wood, then unworked factory grips can usually be obtained. Custom-made grips are also available and the suppliers regularly advertise in the specialist journals. It is not really a difficult job to make one's own grip, but it does take time and patience. It should be remembered that it is the function of the grip that is important not its appearance. An examination of the grips used by top shooters will disclose a great diversity of manufacture and materials. They will consist of a basic piece of wood attached to the frame and built up with plastic wood or plastic filler, added in bits and pieces, until the final product satisfies the shooter. If the final result is aesthetic as well as functional, so much the better.

Before adapting or making the grip the shooter must know the method of gripping. The basic method is to first hold the pistol in the left hand (keeping it clear of the muzzle) using an overhand grip. Then open the right hand, making a 'V' between the thumb and forefinger. The web so formed is placed against the back of the pistol grip, as high up as possible, keeping the fingers extended. Then the second and third fingers are curled round the front of the grip so that middle joints are square. Force will be exerted by the muscles of the hand bringing the pistol grip back against the ball of the thumb. The little finger can curl naturally and be used, if convenient, to assist the other two fingers. However, the thumb must not apply any pressure at all but should sit on the thumb rest at the top of the grip. The thumb rest must be designed so that it takes the thumb in a natural position. The forefinger is used only to release the trigger and will fall naturally on the trigger. To avoid imparting any extraneous movement to the pistol when the trigger is released, no part of this finger must come into contact with the grip. I have seen some shooters gripping laterally between the base of the thumb and the forefinger, thus producing a pinching action at the back of the grip. It is not possible to confirm that this improves the holding of the pistol as it would need to be used early in training and it is probably unwise to change an established routine to examine this hold. The gripping of the pistol is best shown visually (see fig. 5 and plates 1-7). The palm of the hand should make as much contact as possible with the grip, in order to achieve greater control over the pistol.

Some grips are made with thumb holes and extensions to cover the back of the hand, however I do not recommend these. If the back of the hand is in contact with the grip, it will be under some tension which, when the shot is fired, could act as a spring and deflect the pistol from its aim. Similarly the shooter must be careful with palm rests. These should be used

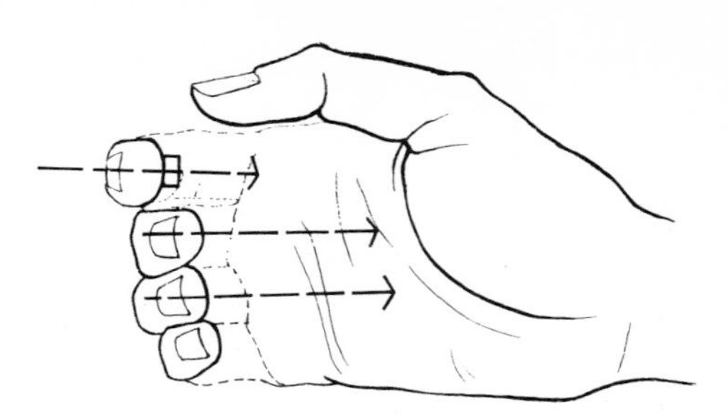

Fig. 5. *Grip: direction of gripping*

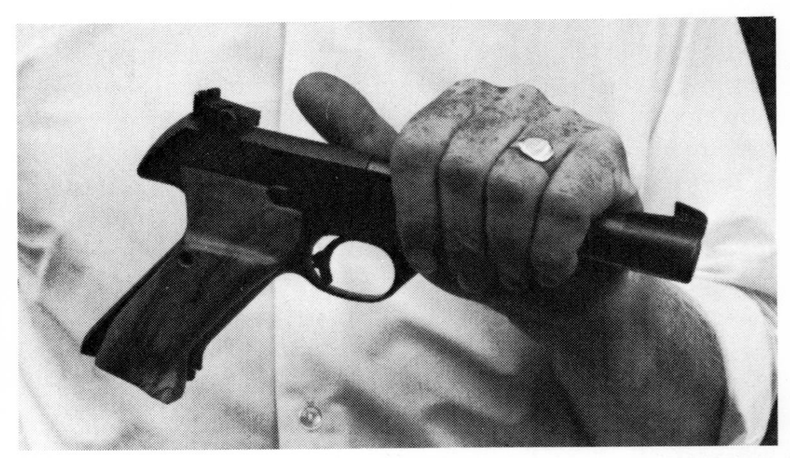

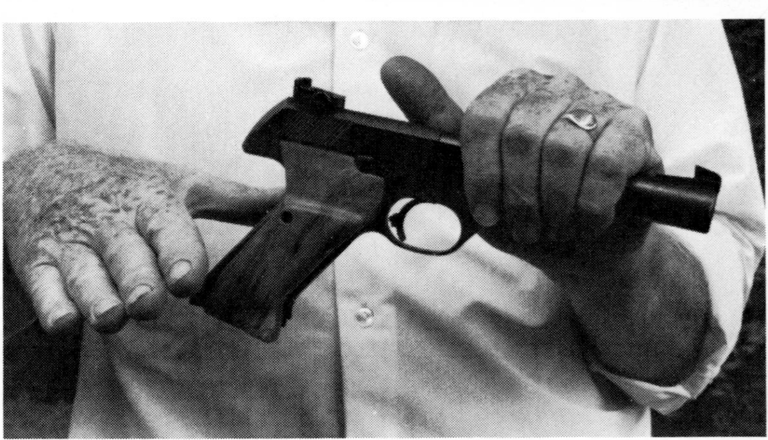

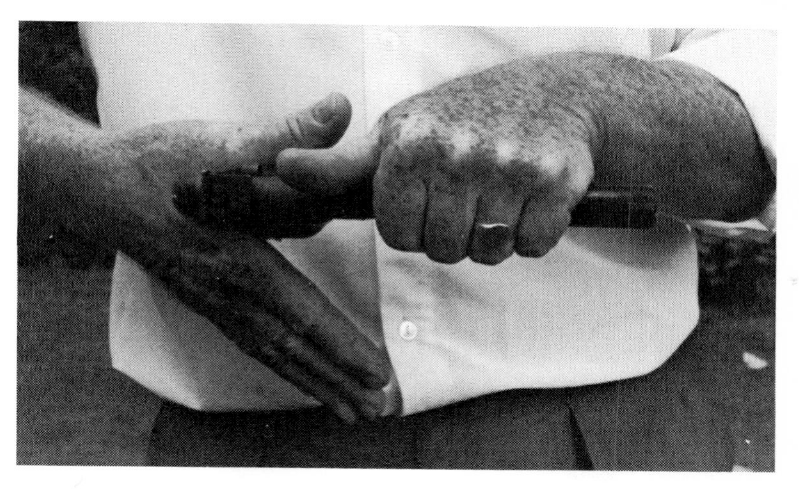

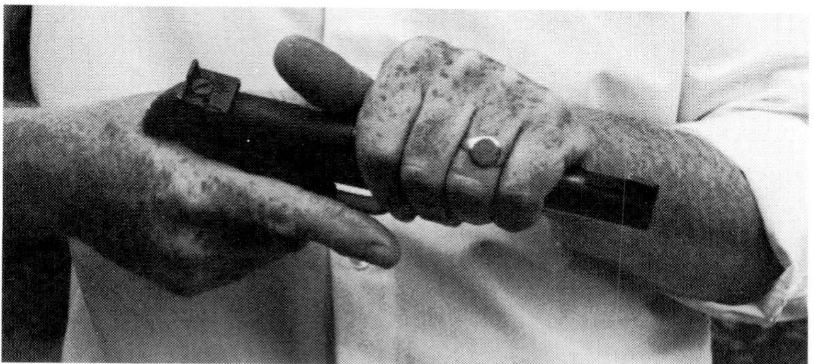

Plates 1 – 5 *Taking the grip*

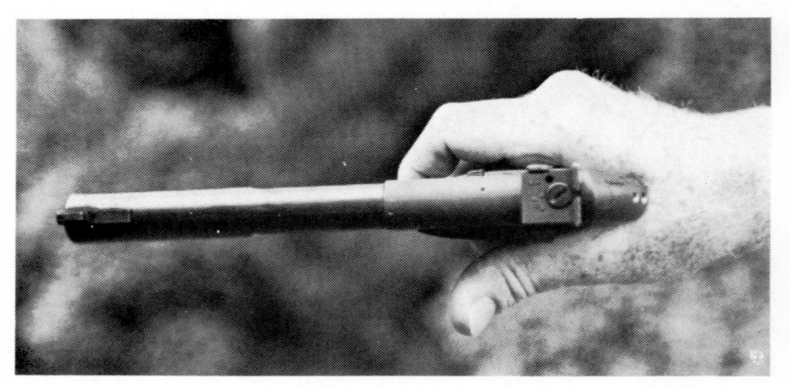

Plates 6 and 7 *Taking the grip*

only to position the hand on the grip and must not squeeze the hand.

When taking the grip, the pad of the forefinger must rest on the bottom of the trigger. The finger must be kept clear of the stock from the knuckle. The trigger release involves complicated muscle co-ordination in the finger and these muscles must be free to react without constriction. (The details of trigger release are described in Chapter 3.) At the moment the pistol is fired, the inside muscles of the trigger finger are contracted and those on the outside are extended. If the inside of the finger is touching the wood there will be some restriction of movement of these muscles. This may also apply to the muscles on the outside of the finger if a 'glove' type of stock is used. At the moment of release the tenseness of the muscles will relax and cause a slight movement. This movement can be transmitted through the pistol causing a slight deflection from the desired aim.

The grip should be taken as high up on the stock as possible. The force of recoil which is taken through the arm should be in line with the arm and so produce no turning movement in a lateral direction. As the line of the barrel is above the hand the turning movement will be in an upwards direction, the movement occurring at the wrist. The higher the hand on the grip the smaller will be the movement. The ideal position would be for the barrel to project from the middle of the hand, therefore producing no turning movement at all, but the rules state that in normal events the barrel must be above the hand. One method which has proved successful is to turn the axis of the pistol through 90°, thus locking the wrist and so preventing any deflecting movement from the recoil. It must have required a long period of training to prove this system. Shooters are always trying to improve their techniques and performances and, as time passes, different ideas will be tried. However the majority of shooters still hold the pistol in the conventional way and the methods discussed here generally relate to the orthodox style.

The most important element in the grip is consistency. One often hears complaints from shooters that their group moves from shoot to shoot and even alters during a shoot so that there is more than one group on the target. Within reason the change of position of the group will not be due to external factors. One should be able to put the pistol away for a considerable time and, when fired again, the group will be in exactly the same place. Changes in group, in my opinion, will be mainly due to slight changes in the grip on the pistol. The grip must be made so that it can be picked up only in exactly the same way each and every time it is used. One must, however, make allowances for changes in temperature. When it is warm the body needs to rid itself of heat, so the blood flows nearer the surface and the hand appears fatter than normal. This will give a tighter fit on the grip. On the other hand, when it is cold the body conserves its heat, the surface blood vessels restrict the flow of blood and the hand feels smaller. This can be partially overcome by keeping the hand as warm as possible — by using a handwarmer or keeping it in a pocket between shots. The shape of the grip will not need to be altered to allow for hot or cold-weather shooting and should be made for average temperature.

Having established the importance of having a grip that can only be held in one way it is now necessary to consider fashioning such a grip. This is a task that any shooter can accomplish (see plates 8-20). The tools required are simple — a small chisel, a Surform (or rasps), abrasive paper and filler. To achieve the basic shape will require a saw, but no great technical skills are necessary. The greatest asset will be patience. One can start with a rough factory stock or find a suitable piece of wood to start from scratch. Suitable wood, such as well-seasoned walnut, is not always easy to find. If such wood is available, buy enough to make three or four grips as it is possible that the first one will not be good enough!

The most important thing to remember about making the grip is that, as the pistol is held at arm's length, any fitting must be made at arm's length. This will involve the co-operation of another person or the use of mirrors set up so that the grip can be examined in the correct position.

As mentioned earlier, the natural shape of the extended arm will determine the approximate angle or rake of the grip. Although the frame of the pistol is at a fixed angle, the grip may (in most pistols) be set at a slightly different angle if necessary. This is best determined by removing the stocks and holding the pistol by the frame in the aiming position. With the help of an assistant the approximate rake of the grip can be estimated. If the old grip is not suitable for alteration then it can be planed down for fitting to the new stock. The hardest part of making a new grip is the fitting to the frame so that it is

8a and 8b Find a suitable piece of well-seasoned wood: usually walnut, but in this case boxwood, which works well and has a nice finish

9 One side cut with tenon saw, then smoothed with plane or glasspaper to fit against frame

10 and 11 Fitting against frame: part to be removed is shaded

12 Excess removed with jig saw, and so shaped and fitted. Next stage is to make thumb rest—portion to be cut back is shaded

13 Cut back for thumb rest

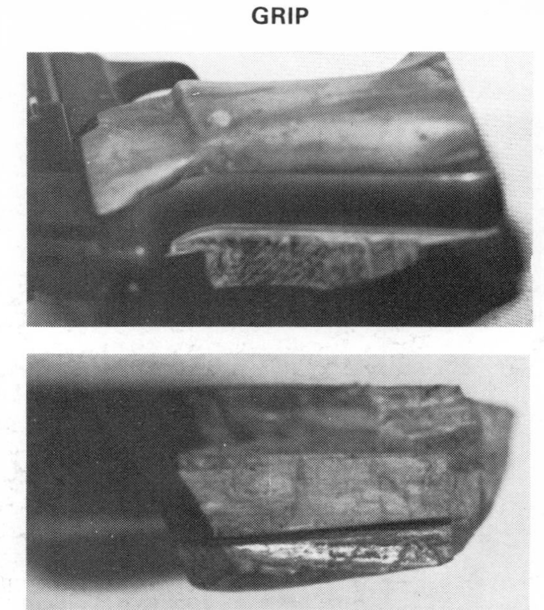

14 and 15 To be thinned so that overall width of frame and both grips does not exceed the regulation width

16 Cut to correct width and marked to show wood to be removed to fit ball of thumb

17 Grip chiselled and smoothed to fit thumb approximately

18 Pencil pointing to part to be pared back for better fit. NB Fitted at arm's length

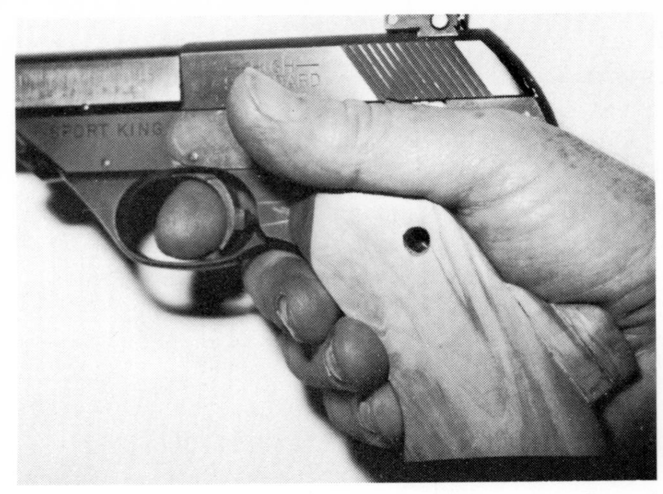

19 Part added to fit under ball of thumb. Thumb resting without pressure; fingers pulling grip back to ball of thumb

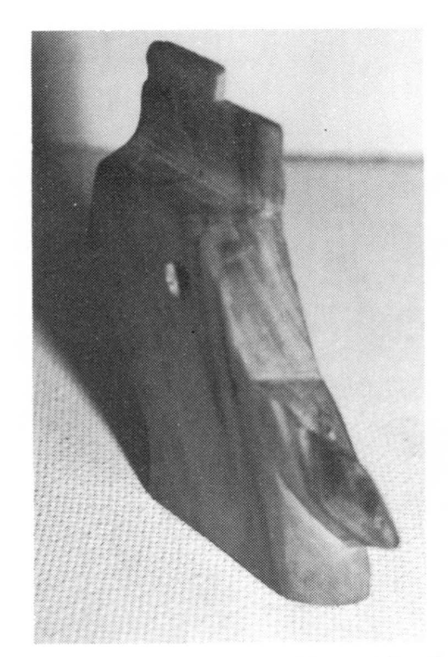

20 Finished grip smoothed down. It will now be fitted to pistol and fired a few times without alteration to check its efficiency

rigid, and using the old grip ensures a good fit. Using a rough factory stock serves the same purpose, but it can be very expensive. If the old stock is used as a basis, the new stock will have to be surface-fitted to it at the right angle. The surfaces can be fitted by rubbing down on abrasive paper on a true surface and then glueing and pinning. If starting with new wood then the old stock can be used as a pattern. One must be very careful when splitting the stock into its two halves. First the width must be determined and, if the stock is asymmetrical, this must be taken into account before making the saw-cut.

Another factor to be considered is the feel of the pistol in the hand. Most shooters prefer to have the pistol barrel heavy, that is, the centre of gravity will be in front of the grip. If a neutral feel is required then the centre of gravity should be at about the position of the trigger. If the former is desired, the grip must be as far forward as possible and if the latter, it is brought back until the pistol feels right. The height of the grip will be determined by the position of the slide, which should just clear the web of the hand between first finger and thumb.

It is probably best to start at the top and work downwards, fitting the web just under the slide and letting the trigger finger fall outside the grip to rest naturally on the trigger. Many triggers are adjustable and so can be fitted to the finger (or vice versa). On the other side of the grip a shelf should be made for the thumb, remembering that when in its rest position the thumb is not flat but slightly tilted to one side. The thumb shelf is normally parallel with the barrel. Having positioned thumb and first finger then the depth of the grip for the other three fingers may be measured and the palm shelf cut out. The front edge may now be fashioned, keeping it as square as possible for the middle joints of the fingers to pull back against the ball of the thumb. All this seems to be very complicated, but the original grip will serve as a model and constant fitting to the hand is essential.

The grip is a functional part of the pistol and so it does not matter if too much wood is removed as it can always be replaced by plastic wood. This is best done by putting on the recommended quantity, covering it with foil or thin plastic and holding it in the aiming position until the surface has set. Then remove the hand and allow the plastic wood to harden. This can be repeated until the shooter is satisfied with the feel of the grip.

The fitting must be comfortable and one must never force the hand into the grip as this will cause tension. The surface of the pistol which is in contact with the hand should be smooth but not polished. The exterior surfaces can of course be polished and decorated according to the whim and skill of the shooter. There is no need to chequer the gripping surfaces of a small-bore pistol, but chequering will assist when holding a centrefire pistol.

When the shooter has apparently finished making the grip it should be used for a time before making any further adjustments. Alterations must never be made in the middle of a shoot. Not only does it disturb neighbouring shooters but it could induce lack of confidence. Adjustments should be made only when there is plenty of time to judge their effect. It is doubtful whether any shooter has made a perfect grip but there is no reason why it should not be more than adequate for him.

The best test for a well-fitting grip is the consistency of position of the group. It is almost certain that any change to the grip will also entail a shift in the position of the group. Before any sight changes are made the shooter should be careful to ensure that the shift of group is due solely to the alterations to the grip and not to external factors. When checking the new grip the pistol should be put down after each shot or, if shooting rapid fire, after each string so that it is picked up afresh. If the groups are consistent then the grip is well fitted.

Alterations can of course be made to the grip already fitted to the pistol, either by removing surplus wood or by adding plastic wood or filler. This, however, does destroy the factory-supplied grips. Even custom-made grips are not always a perfect fit and need some alteration, but they do save a lot of time. This saving of time is, of course, countered by expense!

There are some small points which should be mentioned. In hot weather the hands become both swollen and sweaty. This is not only uncomfortable but also lubricates the grip, making it difficult to take a firm hold. Talc can be used to improve the holding after giving the hands a good wipe with a towel. Nowadays it is not uncommon to see shooters blowing on their hand before holding the pistol. One also sees this in other sports such as tennis and I think it serves two purposes. It helps to remove the film of moisture by evaporation which also cools the hand, therefore affording a better feel on the grip. It might also help the shooter's breathing as the lungs are emptied before taking the couple of deep breaths necessary before firing.

Finally, there is the question of how hard does one grip? The grip should be firm enough to make the pistol an extension of the arm. It should not be possible for another person to move the pistol when held without using excess force. At the same time the grip must not be so firm that tremor is induced. At one time it was held that some pistols should hang from the wrist, but this practice has been superseded and if the pistol is held firmly it should reduce strain on the wrist.

3. Trigger Release

Another basic principle of shooting is trigger release. Various competitions permit different trigger weights from virtually nothing in 'free' weapons to above one kg for other types. Whatever the pressure required to release the trigger, the principle is the same — the trigger must be released smoothly so that the action by the shooter in releasing it does not disturb the aim nor the direction in which the pistol is pointing.

The factors involved are the position and shape of the trigger, its mechanism and the pressure applied by the trigger finger. The position of the finger on the trigger is part of the grip on the pistol (see Chapter 2). The lower the pad of the finger can rest on the trigger the greater the leverage obtained and therefore the greater the control. However, the finger must not be so low that it touches the trigger guard as this will detract from the control. The pad should fall on the trigger at right angles so that the maximum area will be in contact and the trigger can be moved directly backwards in line with the axis of the pistol (see fig. 6). If cared for, the pad is very sensitive and should not be allowed to become calloused and hard. It is not unusual to find hand cream being used to keep the skin soft. One has only to consider the complexity of handwriting to realize how sensitive and flexible the fingers are. Whatever the type of pistol used, the shooter must be able to have his finger in contact with the trigger without any chance of premature release. In my view even with a free pistol the weight on the trigger should not be below twenty grams. In cold weather this will feel very light but still controllable.

When the shooter is ready to fire, a gradually increasing

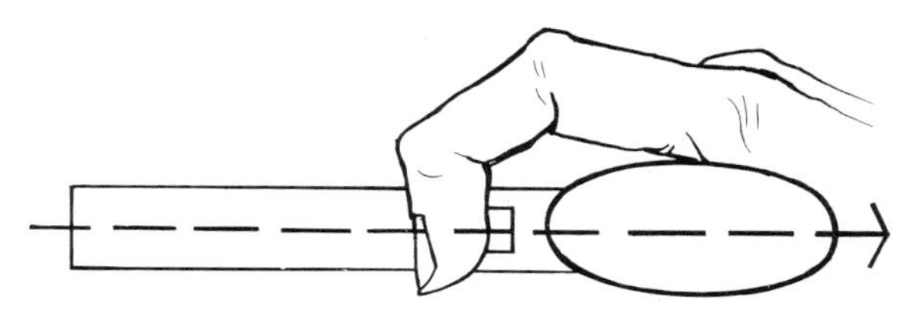

Fig. 6. *Direction of pull and placement of trigger finger*

pressure must be applied to the trigger until the pistol fires. This pressure must be applied directly to the rear so that no side forces deflect the pistol from its correct alignment. If the finger goes too far around the trigger the muzzle will be pulled to the left and if not far enough, the pistol will be pulled to the right. The shot on the target will therefore be off centre, low left or high right. All faults can be demonstrated by the shooter making obvious errors.

Some shooters prefer a quick release of the trigger and others a more gradual release. Whatever the method used, it must be smooth. It is natural when firing a timed shoot for the trigger to be released quickly, but it does not mean that it must be 'snatched'. The release of the trigger is co-ordinated with the other factors and, unless committed to the shot as in rapid fire, it should be possible for the shooter to take his finger off the trigger at the last moment if the other factors do not appear to be right. In timed shoots the shooter must take every preliminary precaution to ensure that he is prepared to fire.

However perfect the operation of the trigger by the shooter any fault in the trigger itself will militate against a good result. The average shooter should know the mechanism of his pistol and be capable of simple maintenance. This will include cleaning the trigger bearings but, unless he is an expert, no attempt should be made to adjust the bearing surfaces as this is a skilled task. The mechanism in a free pistol should be cleaned only by washing in a degreased spirit and should not be stripped. Most trigger mechanisms should be kept dry as oil will attract grit, dust, and grease from cartridges, and malfunctions can occur. The bearing surfaces should break cleanly and any drag should be eliminated.

The final release of the trigger is the most critical part of the shooting process. If the trigger is released when the pistol is pointing in the wrong direction then the whole effort of trying to fire a good shot is wasted. As the trigger release is the last positive act apart from follow-through, it must be considered the vital part of firing the shot.

The trigger should have to travel only a short distance beyond the point of release to avoid disturbance at this time. This can be achieved by installing a trigger stop behind the trigger. It should be adjustable but fitted with lock nuts so that, once set, the shooter should not have to change it. Any competent armourer will undertake such an alteration. A small point to remember is that the screw-head should not protrude from the trigger guard as this could catch on the finger and be a distraction — as well as making it sore!

Some shooters fit a trigger shoe, especially if the trigger is narrow and cannot be felt properly by the finger. Ensure that it is correctly fitted and secure. It can be adjusted for height and the soft metal shaped for the shooter if required.

The release of the trigger is a positive act. It can happen that there will be involuntary release. This is sometimes called a 'surprise' shot and generally occurs during periods of intense concentration when the conscious act is apparently by-passed by the recognition of the correct picture and the trigger is automatically released. Such shots are usually good, but I do not think that the shooter should train to acquire such a skill. The shooter must know that he is in control. There can be no guarantee that the 'surprise' shot technique will occur or succeed every time and it is much better to adopt a tested method and be in positive control.

There is another involuntary release, often described as 'twitch'. This can happen in any part of the body and at any time, more usually when the body is under stress. It cannot be anticipated. Muscular movement is caused by the discharge of electrical potential within the muscle cells. If cells become over charged, an electrical discharge will take place involuntarily. The normal processes of muscular movement are controlled by the nervous system, which will initiate the discharge. When the involuntary action takes place the shooter will be totally unprepared and, if it happens at the moment of firing, the shot may go anywhere and there will be no redress. Precautions can be taken if the shooter is prone to twitch. Gentle exercises such as flexing and unflexing the muscles will help. It is unlikely to happen in timed shoots as these entail the frequent use of muscles and they will not have the opportunity to become over charged.

Follow-through is an integral part of trigger release. Once the trigger releases the tension in the mechanism, the firing pin is forced forward, striking the rim of the cartridge and igniting the primer which in its turn ignites the charge. This creates gases whose pressure in a confined space forces the bullet through the barrel. All this takes time, perhaps only microseconds, during which the pistol must be held still. There will be movement of the pistol when the charge ignites but, if the pistol is held correctly, it will be in line and will not disturb the aim. The gross movement of the pistol which occurs as the bullet leaves the barrel is caused by the gases expanding into the air. It is at this point too, that the greatest noise is heard. The pistol must be held on aim throughout this time, for by maintaining the aim the pistol will come to rest (after the shocks of recoil and discharge have been absorbed) pointing at the spot where it was aimed at the moment of firing. This will give a good guide to the quality of the shot (as will be explained later). If the pistol is held on aim through the shot there will be no thought of lowering the pistol to the bench too soon. How often one sees a shooter trying to use his telescope before the shot has reached the target! If the pistol is lowered so quickly, the intention, and therefore the executive thought processes, must have been there before the shot was fired. The concentration on firing the shot is therefore bound to have deteriorated, with the predictable consequence of an uncertain shot. The intention to lower the pistol must not be initiated until the shot has been fired. Thus there are very good reasons for including a good follow-through in the shooter's technique.

Trigger freeze is the inability to physically release the trigger when the sight picture seems correct. It stems from the fear of firing a poor shot. The message from the brain to the trigger finger is blocked en route and although the mental impression is that of trying to release the trigger, nothing is happening. If then the message does get through there is likely to be a hasty release of the trigger or snatch with a probable poor shot. If trigger freeze does arise, the pistol should be brought down, the technique thought through and another attempt made with a positive approach that the shot will be a good one.

Mechanical defects can occur in trigger mechanisms. Careful watch must be kept on the feel of the trigger and it should be tested at frequent intervals if it has to carry a prescribed weight. In a competition, triggers are tested prior to the match and may be tested during a match if the officials so desire, but on no account should the shooter be disturbed whilst firing a shot. A trigger test only indicates the state of the trigger at that moment. A trigger might be tested before the last shot of a competition and pass the test, but not take the weight after the last shot. This will only indicate the condition of the pistol at that moment and such a test should not be retrospective.

4. The Aim

Having adopted a proper stance and gripped the pistol correctly, the step before releasing the trigger is to take a good aim. This is probably the most controversial part of pistol shooting as there are differing ideas as to what constitutes a good aim.

The object of the aim is to align the sights so that the shot fired hits the centre of the target. A series of shots is called a group and the mean point of impact (M.P.I.), the centre of the group, should be the centre of the target. Modern pistols have adjustable backsights and usually a variety of interchangeable foresights. The backsights can be adjusted both vertically and laterally and the method of adjustment will enable precise alterations to be made. The instructions with the pistol will define how much the M.P.I. will be changed by rotating the adjusting screws. The shooter must keep a note of the changes that each of his pistols needs, both for range and also for vertical and lateral movements at each range. He should also note in which direction the screws should be rotated to move the sights in the desired direction. This note should be put in a prominent place in his notebook or displayed in his pistol box. There are still in use a number of pistols without easily adjustable sights but the basic principles for aiming remain the same.

The elements involved in the aim are the target, the front or foresight, the rear or backsight, and the eye. The pistol will be aligned so that the point of aim, the tip of the foresight, the shoulders of the backsight, and the eye are in the same horizontal plane. The vertical plane will pass through the vertical axis of the target, the centre of the tip of the foresight, the centre of the notch in the rearsight and the eye. When these two planes cross, the pistol will be correctly aligned and if fired at that time, provided the other principles have been adhered to, a shot will fall within the shooter's group.

The eye is the most important element in aiming. It is an optical instrument which concentrates the light it receives on the retina by means of a fluid lens capable of altering its focal length by muscular control, and thus enabling objects at all distances to be clearly seen. The retina converts the light received into electrical impulses which when passed to the brain are translated into visual images. In the light of experience the brain will interpret what it sees and, when the aim is judged correct, initiate the firing procedures. If the images are not clear then the eye needs examination by a qualified person to show whether corrective lenses will enable the shooter to see clearly at the required distance.

The eye cannot focus at three different distances simultaneously, therefore the target, the foresight and rearsight cannot all be in sharp focus at the same time. The target does not move between shots and once the direction of the shot is determined, by taking the correct stance, this, too, does not change. The shape of the target will appear constant, even though slightly out of focus, but its density may change according to the brightness of the ambient light. However, for practical purposes it appears unchanged. The backsight should be looked *through*, its presence assumed rather than seen, in order to determine the foresight position in relation to the backsight. It is most important for the foresight to be in sharp focus, so that it can be accurately positioned within the framework of the backsight. If the shooter has really keen eyesight and good concentration he can pinpoint part of the foresight, e.g. its tip or, even better, its top corner. The better the muscular control the smaller will be the arc of movement made by the muzzle of the pistol. Any movement of the foresight in relation to the backsight will be more easily seen if the foresight is in sharp focus, and therefore more easily controlled.

If the foresight cannot be focused corrective glasses will probably be required. When visiting the optician it is necessary to take a pistol, so that the shooter can demonstrate what is required and measurements can be taken from the eye to the foresight in order to calculate the correct prescription. If the optician says that glasses are needed, the shooter will have to decide which shooting glasses he will acquire so that the correct size of lenses can be made to fit the holders. Before the lenses are made, the optician should have the opportunity to see the frame, as they may stand out from the eye a little further than normal frames and thus change the prescription. Advice should also be sought about filters for use in either bright light or dull conditions (see plate 21). Some shooters use chrome filters in dull light as these brighten up the background. Grey or blue filters can be used in bright light to reduce the intensity. However it should be remembered that any filter will reduce the amount of light that enters the eye. A further factor to be considered is whether *all* the light is

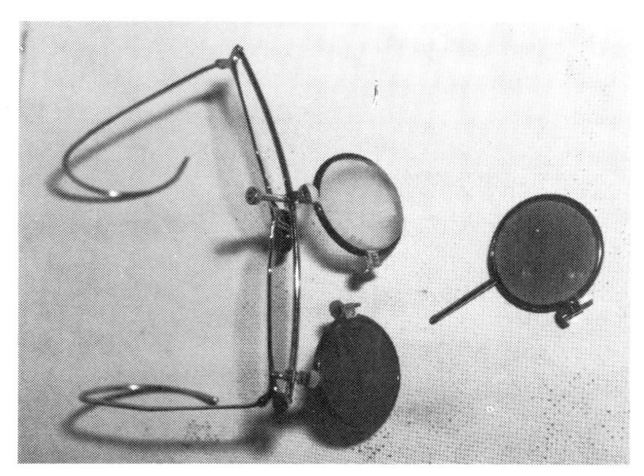

21 Author's Knobloch shooting glasses with spare filter for bright light. The aiming lenses both have fixed apertures

allowed into the eye or only that central portion which will envisage the sights and target area. Various sizes of aperture can be obtained with the shooting glasses and it is wise to try more than one to find which is most suitable. With most shooting glasses it is possible to obtain a variable iris, and it is advisable to use the largest comfortable aperture. If the aperture is too small insufficient light will reach the eye and the eye will strain to use what light is available. The iris should therefore be stopped down until there is insufficient light and then opened up to the required size.

Only one eye will see the aim, the other does not see the detail and is only concerned with perspective. To avoid strain to the aiming eye the other eye should remain open; if one eye is shut this will try to open, and vice versa, and an avoidable strain is introduced. The best way is to use binocular vision, but this requires training at an early stage. It is possible to change from monocular to binocular vision but it is difficult and the shooter may revert at an awkward moment. In monocular aiming, the inhibited eye can be covered by a plain translucent lens, so that light enters the eye enabling it to remain open without strain. Polaroid lenses can be used for this purpose.

Even if the shooter does not require corrective glasses he can take measures to facilitate the sharp focusing of the foresight. This involves the use of an aperture (or iris) which can be fixed to ordinary plain lenses. These should be of safety glass made to an optical specification. One type of variable aperture fits to the lens by a small suction cup. It is fitted to the lens in the aiming position so that it is correctly placed in the line of sight. A shooter may, however, prefer to make his own aperture by marking on the lens the point which coincides with the line of sight. A patch is then affixed with a good round hole at the correct spot. The other lens can be covered with a white paper or rubbed with abrasive paper to make it opaque. Glasses also have a safety factor. An examination of a pair of well-used shooting glasses will show small pit marks caused by small fragments from the breech which, but for the glasses, might have hit the eyes.

It is worthwhile considering dominant eyes. Most people have a dominant eye — one that perceives the detail whilst the other adds the perspective. This is usually the same as their laterality so that right-handed people have a dominant right eye. It can happen that the opposite eye is dominant and this means that the pistol has to be brought across to line up with the eye. This causes a greater angle at the wrist, where the recoil will induce a greater turning motion and therefore the pistol will be harder to control. The grip will have to take into account the greater angle so that the axis of the grip will not coincide with the axis of the pistol. This is not a simple operation. The shooter has to choose whether to shoot with his dominant eye or whether to adopt the orthodox technique and shoot with his other eye. I am right-handed and have a dominant left eye but I shoot with my right eye, considering the advantage of the stance and line of sight to outweigh the advantage of shooting with the stronger eye. For this purpose there is really very little difference between the eyes, but an eye defect may leave no option about which method to adopt. It is wise to have a periodic eye-check, especially if the shooter does seem to have difficulty in focusing.

Returning to the method of aiming, the correct sight relationship is that the foresight will appear within the notch of the backsight with its top level with the shoulders of the backsight (see fig. 7). There must be an equal amount of light through the notch of the backsight on either side of the foresight. There has always been discussion on the most suitable width of the foresight and, consequently, on the width of the backsight notch. The narrower the foresight, the harder the pistol will appear to control as even slight movements will be accentuated. On the other hand, too wide a foresight will be difficult to place on the required point of aim. A reasonable compromise is that the width of the foresight should be about the same apparent width of the aiming mark.

This will enable the sight relationship to maintain a better position *vis-à-vis* the aiming mark. Whatever widths are adopted the shooter must avoid eyestrain caused by trying to focus on too narrow a foresight. The width of the backsight notch should be about twice that of the foresight (as seen in the aim) and its depth the same as the apparent width of the foresight.

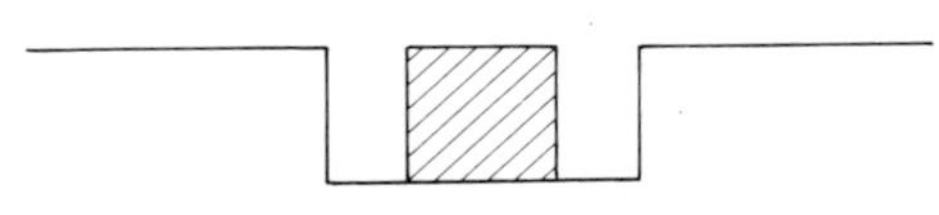

Fig. 7. *Sight relationship*

Various shapes of foresight are made, but generally speaking the target shooter will prefer a sight which presents a square image to the eye. As the eye will see any small irregularity, the foresight should be inspected at frequent intervals to see that it does not become loose or damaged. If damaged, any small burrs should be removed with a fine file or stone to restore the square shape.

To avoid reflection which will distort the apparent shape of the foresight it should be treated before the shoot by applying carbon black. This is best produced on the range by an acetylene flame which gives a very fine black. Try to avoid looking directly at the flame as the eye will take a little while to recover from the effect of the very intense light.

Before applying the black, the sights should be cleaned to provide a smooth surface. The black must be applied to all surfaces of the sight and to the barrel, if that comes into the shooter's view when aiming. Even when shooting against a black target, as in rapid fire, it is important to have a well-blacked sight. Proprietory liquid black can be bought but may give an uneven surface unless very carefully applied. In an emergency an ordinary match will provide sufficient black.

The sight relationship having been defined, the next step is to discuss the sight picture, i.e. what the eye sees when looking through the sights at the target and focusing on the foresight (see fig. 8). For the purpose of discussion it will be assumed that the aiming mark is a black disc on a white target, the usual type of target except for rapid fire. The correct sight relationship has to be seen against the target so that the eye can see a pattern that will be repeated time after time. Because it is reproduced frequently the brain will recognize it as the correct sight picture. When that pattern is recognized as correct the picture must be maintained while the trigger is released. It is generally accepted that the point of aim will be below the aiming mark into the white and the amount of white will depend on the individual shooter.

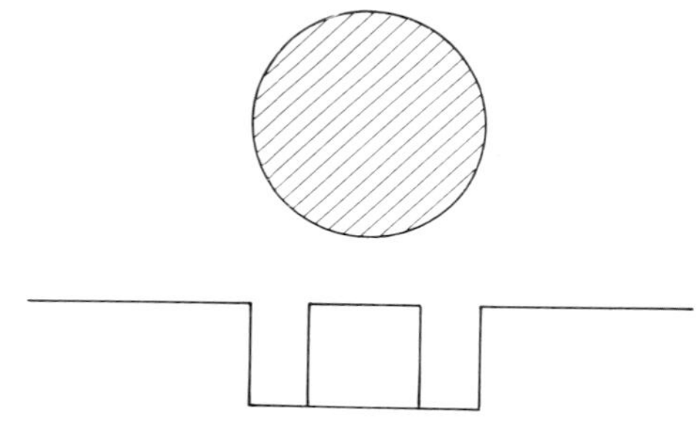

Fig. 8. *Sight picture*

As there will always be some movement at the muzzle due to natural movements within the body it will be impossible for a point aim to be held. The point of aim will wander within the grouping capacity of the shooter and it is therefore undesirable to aim at the aiming mark itself. A centre aim is very difficult to hold as one is setting a black sight against a black background and obscuring part of the reference point. It is impossible to hold a group smaller than the natural group induced by minimal movements within the body and magnified by the length of the arm.

The general area of aim will therefore fall below the aiming mark. The eye will see a strip of white between the aiming mark and the top of the foresight and will learn to recognize how big or how little that strip should be (see fig. 9). I prefer a

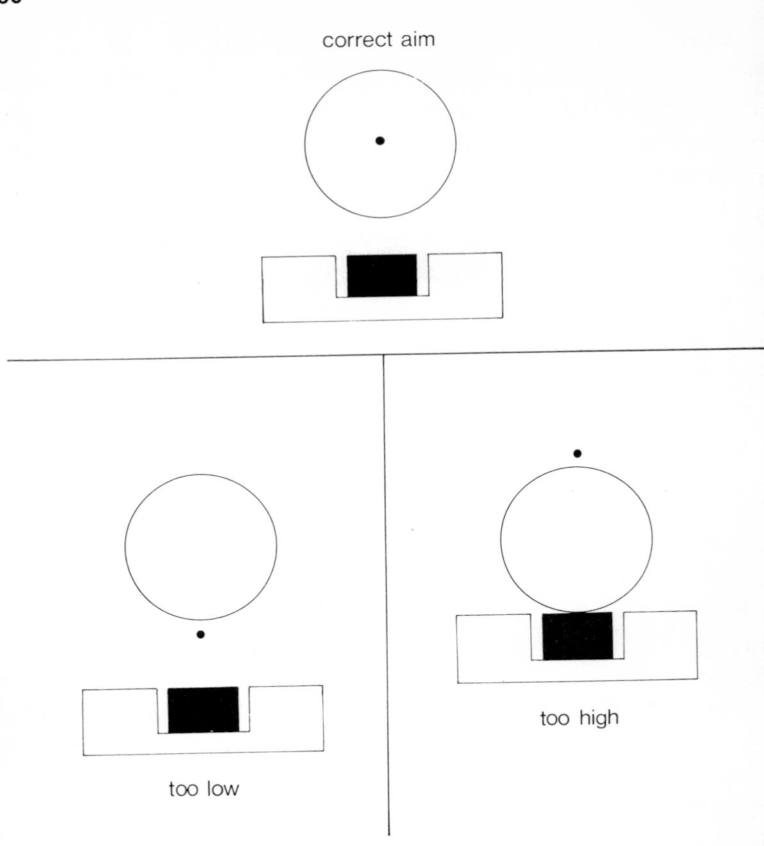

Fig. 9. *Sight pictures*

fairly large strip, so that the eye is not drawn to the aiming mark but remains focused on the foresight. If the aim is too close to the aiming mark the eye can occasionally switch from the foresight to the aiming mark, changing the point of aim and therefore firing a shot outside the proper group. The aiming mark will normally appear slightly indistinct; if it suddenly becomes clearer and the foresight loses its sharpness it will be because the eye is looking at the target and not at the sights. The fuzzy target will look the same each time but it will not move, unlike the pistol which will have a little movement.

With the aiming point well down the target, the aim will become an area aim and the muzzle will move about in a small area. If the sight relationship is correct any movement will be within the grouping capacity of the shooter and any shots outside that area will not be a sighting error. Assuming the shooter can keep all his shots within the '8' ring then his sight picture can move within an '8' ring circle around his normal point of aim and so all shots will fall within the '8'. As the skill of the shooter develops, the area of movement will decrease, the group will become smaller and the score will become higher. Although the area of aim is well below the aiming mark, the group can be positioned in the centre of the target by altering the sights. Sights are put on a pistol to be used. A shooter should never try and adjust the position of his group by aiming off. Although it may work for the odd shot it is most unreliable.

Each make of pistol has a slightly different way of altering the backsight ranging from simple screws to precise, spring-loaded screws giving so much movement per click. Front-sights are generally fixed and will only be altered if a different width is desired or if the adjustment of the backsight is close to its extremity and a bigger or shorter frontsight is needed. The general principle to remember is that if the backsight is raised the group is raised and vice versa. Laterally, if the backsight is moved to the right then the shots will move to the right and if to the left then the shots will move left (see figs. 10 and 11). Thus it is necessary to move the sights in the direction in which the group needs to go. Sight alteration should be a part of training so that the shooter learns how to adjust his sights and what effect any changes will cause. Sight alterations should not be made on the results of a single shot but once a group has formed (this can be a minimum of three shots). One could fire a shot which is at the right-hand edge of the group, the shooter applies correction and his next shot may be very left (if this shot had originally been at the left-hand edge of his normal group with the addition of the applied correction). This will result in a constant chasing of errors with disastrous

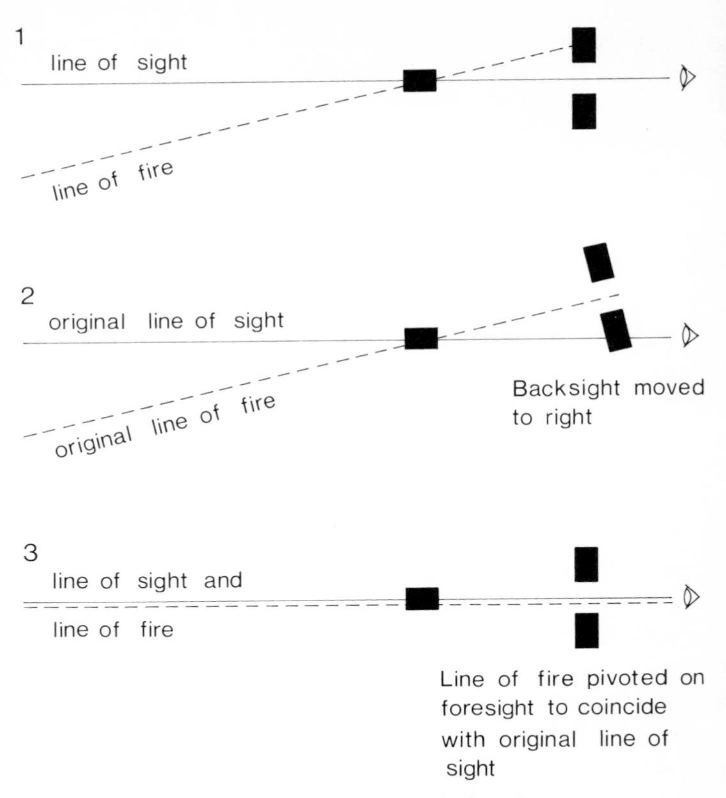

Fig. 10. *Correction of direction*

results. If a change is needed it is best to overestimate the change. If the shooter thinks that two clicks (of the adjustable screws) are needed then he should adjust by three clicks. However shooters will seldom need to change sights during a shoot as alterations should have been made during the sighting period. There may be slight differences between indoor and outdoor shooting and between bright days and dull days. The shooter should be aware of how light conditions affect him and be prepared to make the necessary adjustments early.

Lateral alterations will seldom be necessary, unless a fresh to strong wind is encountered. The problem here will not be one of sighting, but mainly of the effect of the wind on the

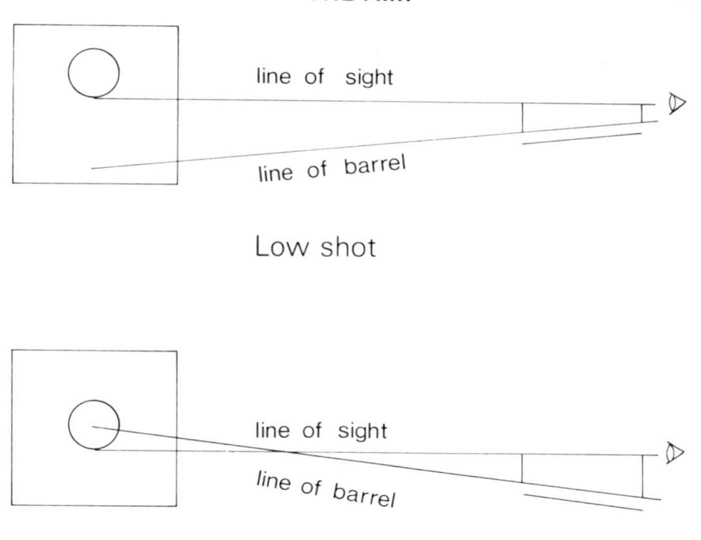

Same foresight : higher backsight

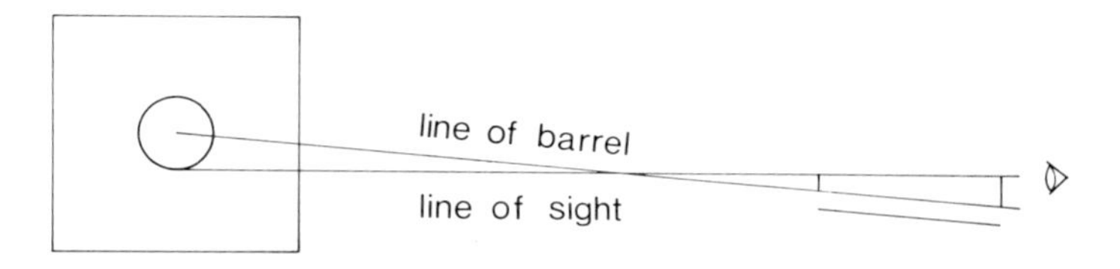

Shorter foresight : same backsight

Fig. 11. *Correction of elevation*

outstretched arm. If the wind is constant the shooter gets accustomed to it and is often caught out when the wind slackens or stops at the moment of trigger release — the result being a shot downwind. Wind will seldom make a sight alteration of more than three clicks. Light can affect lateral

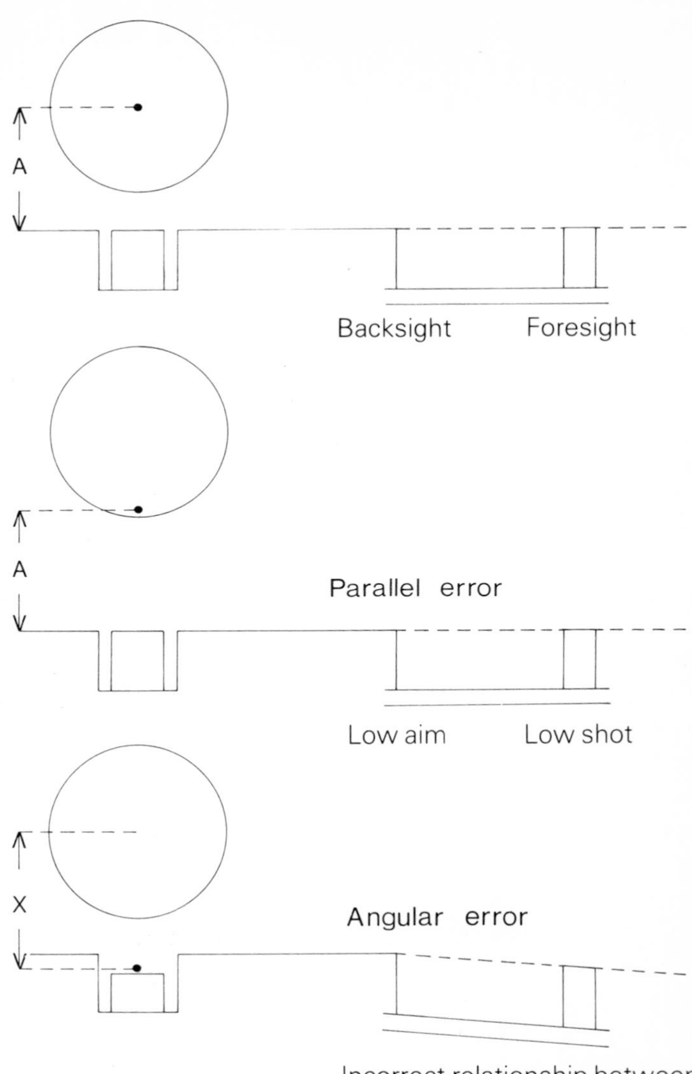

Fig. 12. *Relation between parallel and angular errors*

movement, especially when it is coming from the side early or late in the day. It will illuminate one side of the foresight and bring the other side into shadow. This will have the effect of moving the foresight in the direction of the light and may warrant a sight change of two to three clicks.

The shooter should make a record of any sight changes at the time, so that at the end of the shoot he can return the sights to their proper zero; that is the setting at which, under normal conditions, the group will be centrally placed.

The majority of errors on the target will be in sighting. It can be hard to concentrate on the foresight throughout a long match and if a shot is fired when the foresight is not clear then the accuracy of that shot is in doubt. If the sight relationship is maintained, the shot will strike the target at a point the same distance from the centre of the target as the sight was from the centre of the aiming area. This is known as a parallel error (see fig. 12). If, however, the sight relationship is not maintained then the angle of the sight and barrel is altered and the hit will not bear any relationship to the group and sighting area. As such errors are within the sight base the effect on the target will be great. The sight base varies from six to ten inches and even a small error in this distance will assume larger proportions on the target. Angular sight errors can be illustrated and it is useful for the shooter to deliberately fire a series of shots to demonstrate to himself their effect (see fig. 13).

It is therefore important to maintain the correct sight relationship in order to reduce errors due to sight misplacement. It is worthwhile noting at this point that whereas a coach can see the stance, the grip, and the trigger release, he cannot see the shooter's sight picture and must rely on the shooter giving him an honest answer about the aim. If the shooter finds it difficult to maintain the correct sight relationship it could be due to an incorrect stance or an incorrectly aligned grip. The latter should be checked both with regard to the alignment of the grip *vis-à-vis* the axis of the pistol and to the grip the hand is taking of the stock. If the group tends to be lateral, one cause can be too much lateral movement in the

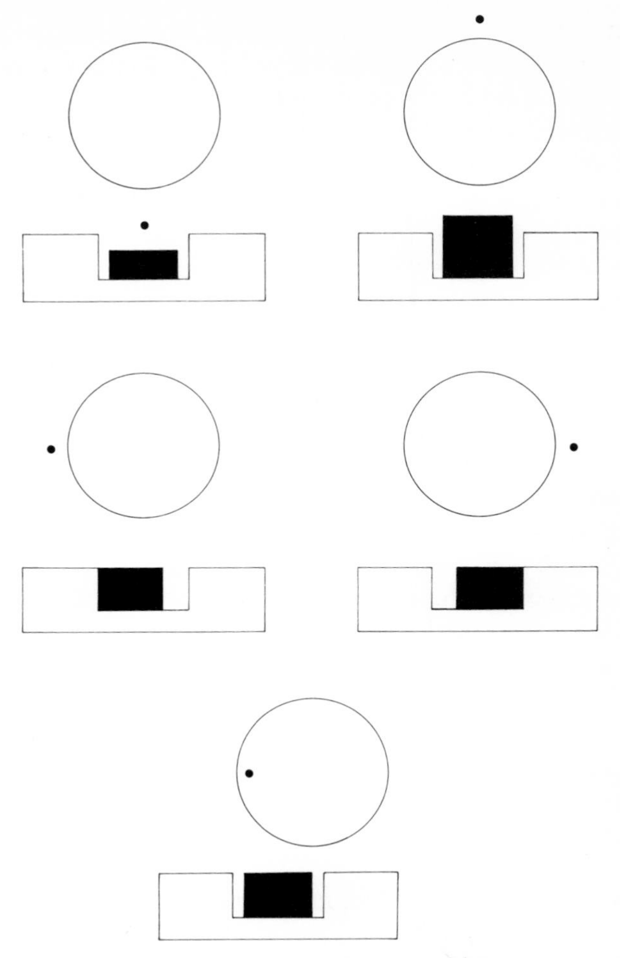

Fig. 13. *Aiming errors*

sight picture. This may be overcome by moving the sight picture up and down — through the centre of the aiming point and in a decreasing arc — until the sights settle at the aiming point, then the trigger is released.

One of the best methods of checking sighting errors is to shoot on a white target, i.e. turn a target back to front so that there is no aiming mark to distract from the sight picture. The eye will naturally bisect the target vertically, but will be unable to accurately bisect on the horizontal plane because part of the target will be obscured by the sights. The group will therefore be narrow but long in the vertical axis. Such a group can be evaluated by making a template from another target (see fig. 14). The target can be separated into strips as illustrated and placed over the group. It will often be found that such a group is narrower than that which the shooter normally fires when shooting for a score. Such practice will show up errors in zero, sight relationship and trigger release. The error in zero will be shown if the group is displaced laterally. Shots outside the normal group of the shooter will be due to sighting errors or faulty trigger release. Shot calling by the shooter and observation by the coach will enable the error to be specified.

The following dry firing exercise can be carried out at home, always observing safety precautions. A small ring on the wall at the appropriate height is all that is required. The size of the

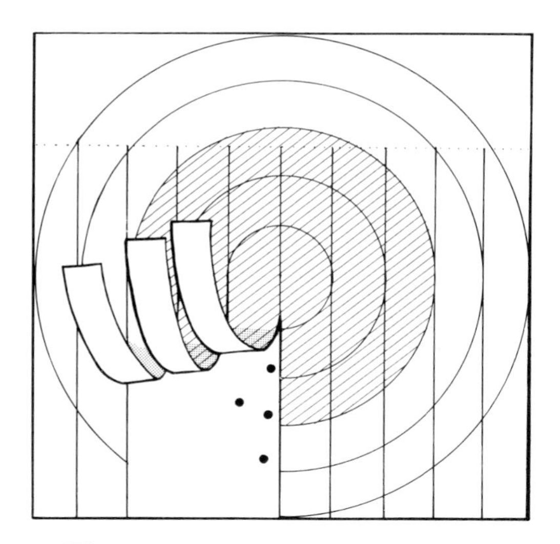

Fig. 14. *Template for blank target*

ring will depend on the skill of the shooter. Initially it should be large enough for the aim to be held within the ring. As the shooter's skill increases so the diameter of the ring can be reduced. The practice should not be overdone, and should be limited to about twenty shots fired within the ring. The concentration on this dry firing is as important as with live firing, otherwise it will be a waste of effort and time. A 'that is good enough' approach in training will instil the wrong attitude which will be carried over into live firing. As the skill improves, not only can the number of shots be increased, but the length of hold can be extended beyond that which is required to fire the shot. This will encourage a good follow-through. This is training that can be done in the shooter's spare time, and spare time is precious. By making it a regular routine there will be an element of self-discipline which is important to success.

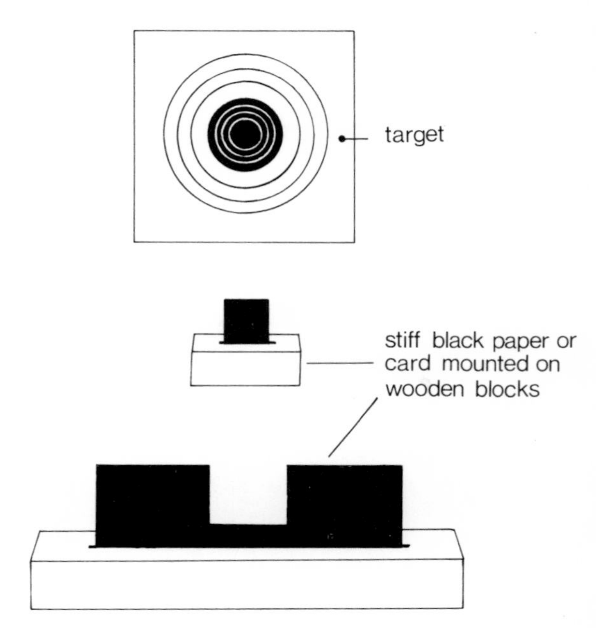

Fig. 15. *Model for demonstrating aim*

Whereas the other elements can be demonstrated by the coach the aim can be demonstrated only by diagrams and models, such as using a pole on which are mounted stiff paper models of the foresight and backsight. This must be capable of being held stationary so that the sight relationship can be set up first by the coach and then by the pupil in order that both understand what the other is seeing. It is not beyond the wit of the average individual to make such a model (see fig. 15) to use in coaching and training sessions.

5. Applying the Principles

Pistol shooting is not a number of separate actions but the co-ordination and fusion of the parts. Having considered the more important elements, the next step is to consider the actions to be taken before and on the range to bring them together.

Some additional equipment will be required and a walk along any firing point will show the variety available. The pistol or pistols must be carried from home to range and vice versa and often the box used is put on the bench to support other equipment. However in some competitions, such as rapid fire, benches are not used and therefore the specialist shooter will adapt his requirements to his own specification.

The shooter will need in addition to his weapon, ammunition, cleaning equipment and some basic tools. Each shooter will collect his own impedimenta, but the experienced will gradually eliminate unnecessary items because of their weight. A few spare parts, such as a firing pin, will be useful, but each shooter will know which parts are likely to need replacing in an emergency. Usually, there will be someone on the range who will give assistance when the shooter does not have the right spare part or tool.

It is usual for each shooter to have his own telescope. There are many excellent models on the market and the actual one chosen will depend on requirements and price. For smallbore shooting the telescope should be able to distinguish shot holes at fifty metres. It should be light, capable of focusing down to ten metres, and small enough to fit into the shooter's box. It will have to stand on the bench on a suitable tripod or be clamped to the box. In all cases the shooter will adjust the position of the eyepiece so that he does not have to disturb his stance to use the telescope. There should also be room in the box for the shooting glasses and a cap with a long peak and side flaps to shield the eyes from bright sunlight.

One of the more important items of additional equipment will be ear protectors. It has been shown that pistols, being short-barrelled, produce a more intense shock wave than rifles. This shock wave will cause permanent damage to the ear if steps are not taken to reduce the effects. There are now many ear protectors available. The most common resemble external muff-like headphones. These filter out the damaging waves but allow the shooter to hear range commands and other conversation. The use of empty cartridge cases or cotton wool is of very little benefit, but ear plugs are effective if used exactly as prescribed. They are probably a better form of protection for spectators than for shooters. Protectors should be inspected for damage from time to time and should be kept clean. Another advantage of using ear protectors is that they help concentration by reducing distraction from external noise.

A notebook and pencil must be kept in the box. Most shooters like to keep a detailed record of their shoots, shot by shot. Commercial score books are available but individual methods are often used. Any method of recording is worthwhile provided it is for a purpose. It should be examined to see what progress is being made and what parts of a shoot are better than others. By recording the pattern of the shots, the shape of the group can be determined and possible errors in technique discovered. The record should *not* be used as a watch on the score. The score is the empirical assessment of the group and any thoughts on how well or how badly the shoot is progressing will detract from the purpose in hand, that is, to fire the next shot or series of shots. It is arbitrary whether the shoot is of ten shots or twenty-seven. The concern of the shooter is to make his group as small as possible. He will know when he fires whether the shot was a good one or not, without looking through the telescope. It should, however, be used carefully during the sighting session when the shooter reminds himself of his technique, examines the conditions and checks that his group is in the centre (if not, he adjusts the sights). During the actual shoot a glance through the telescope every two or three shots should suffice to keep a check on the position of the group.

Other items to be carried by the shooter should include a cloth for keeping the hands dry. The grip should not become moist as it could then slip in the hand. If the weather is very hot some talc is useful to absorb the perspiration. Another cloth or pad to put on the bench to protect the pistol from abrasion does not add unnecessary weight. The rule book should be carried, but the shooter should have studied the rules carefully before competing. It is the responsibility of the shooter to be conversant with the rules, and any breach of them cannot be mitigated by professing ignorance.

Finally, it will be no good carrying all this equipment if the ammunition is forgotten! There should be sufficient of the same batch to cover all matches and practices, with some over for emergencies. Careful shooters will have checked each round to see that it does not carry excess grease, and that if it does most of it is wiped off. Too much grease will build up around the breech and eventually will result in malfunctions (see also Chapter 9). A spent match or toothpick is useful in removing hard grease as it will not scratch the metal.

Having dressed in appropriate clothing, the shooter will check in at the range. Unless there has been a preliminary weapon check there will almost certainly be one before the match. If the shooter has studied his rules there will be no fear of his pistol failing to pass any test, although he should always expect strict interpretation of the rules. If the pistol has to lift a certain weight, he should have given it frequent checks. He will also have made sure that no equipment has been left behind. A check list in the pistol box will help. If the occasion is an international or important team match the coach will help the shooter to present himself to his firing point in the right frame of mind. The shooter will take his place on the previously allotted firing point and, assuming that there is a bench or table, will set up his equipment. If not, he will put his equipment in the space provided behind the firing point and make his preparations there. The shooter will mount his telescope for the precision shoot, but in timed shoots a telescope is not normally allowed. The telescope will be positioned so that, when the correct stance is adopted, a head movement alone will allow the shooter to use it. Care must be taken that there is no danger of any part of the shooter or his clothing coming into contact with his telescope, box or table. He will take out of his box his immediate requirements, such as the pistol, magazine(s), ammunition, the cloth to rest the pistol on and one to keep his hands dry. He may also unpack his notebook and pencil, and a stopwatch to check on the unexpired time for shooting. A tool for adjusting sights should be handy. The shooter will check his sights to ensure that all is in order (see Chapter 4). However, none of these preparations may take place until the range officer has given permission for the shooter to take up his place, and a shooter must obey all subsequent orders. Finally, the shooter will set out his shooting glasses (inspecting them to see that they are clean), the ear defenders and cap (if required). Having made sure that all is in order the shooter should go through his technique in his imagination, study the range conditions, relax, and wait for the range officer to give the next order.

An order to load will be given. Depending on the rules in force, this will either mean load the magazine (if a self-loading pistol is being used) or insert the loaded magazine into the pistol, or put a round into the chamber of a single-shot pistol. It is important that the shooter knows the rules and has established whether there are any local variations. He may now take up the stance that suits him, take a proper grip on the pistol, look at the target, close the eyes and raise the pistol to try his aim. When the arm is raised to the aiming position it is usually taken up above the centre of the target and then allowed to drop to the required level. This overcomes any resistance in the muscle joints and loosens the clothes so that they are comfortable. The eyes are then opened and the first observed position of the aim in relation to the vertical axis should be noted. Adjustments to the stance can be made (as previously described) until the shooter is satisfied. Whether the shooter is a novice or very experienced, he must take the stance that is best for him at the time, remembering that the shorter the distance the more care must be taken with the stance. The routine of taking up the position must become established and be part of the preparation that gives the shooter confidence. It eliminates many of the possible variables which can affect the shape and position of the group. (Of course, prior to taking his trial stance, the shooter will have put on his spectacles, his shooting cap and his ear protectors.)

Once the order to 'fire' or 'commence' has been given the shooter is at liberty to fire the shot. Unless it is a timed shoot, when the shooter himself declares when he is ready, the firing commences on the command of the range officer. As I described in *Modern Pistol Shooting* there is an optimum time when all the factors involved reach their peak. This peak lasts for a second or two during which the best overall results are obtained. There are always exceptions to every rule and some shooters can get good results when holding for a longer period. However, I think that if the pistol is held on aim beyond a certain period the chance of a good shot diminishes, and there is no room for taking chances in this sport. I have no reason to alter my previous criteria and will therefore paraphrase from that book. The four factors involved are breathing, trigger control, ability to hold and concentration.

The breathing has to be restrained, although there are modern theories that suggest the shooter should breathe *through* the shot, except at the moment of release. However, the more usual method is to take a couple of deep breaths when ready to lift the pistol from the bench. The whole body depends on an ample supply of oxygen to release energy from stored chemicals in the cells. If the breathing has to be restrained the blood must be enriched first, hence the need for the deep breathing. The untrained shooter must, however, take care as deep breathing can cause fainting unless the body is fit. The breath can be held for quite a long time but here we are concerned with a minimum time in which the body can continue to make a peak effort without apparent breathing. The purpose of restraining the breathing is to avoid the movement to the arm caused by the motion of the chest as the lungs are filled and emptied. It is estimated that the peak effort can be maintained for about ten seconds but, if the shooter is well trained, this can be longer. The method of restraining the breathing is to take two deep breaths then to allow the air to leave the lungs until no strain is felt. This means that the lungs are now about half full and the pressure of the atmosphere is balanced by the rest position of the muscles which operate the chest and diaphragm. A noticeable sign that the breath is being held too long is an increase in the pulse with a consequent movement of the muzzle of the pistol in a wider and wider arc. Therefore, as far as this factor is concerned, the sooner the shot is fired the better.

A time factor is also included in trigger control. If the trigger is fired too quickly it will be 'snatched', or jerked, and not pulled back in a smooth continuous movement. If the aim has been held too long the shooter will try to get the shot away when he thinks the aim is about right and again will operate the trigger too quickly. However, a gradual increasing pressure on the trigger will coincide with the gradual improvement of the sight picture and the shot will be fired when the sight picture is held within the grouping area of the shooter. This is between six and ten seconds. Of course, timed fire will have different criteria, but the same factors apply. For instance, in rapid fire, or any timed shoot up to ten seconds, the breath can be restrained throughout the shoot. In longer timed shoots a quick change of air will be worthwhile.

The third factor is the efficiency of the muscles being used to hold the body upright and the pistol at arm's length. Muscles do become fatigued under stress. It is quite obvious to the shooter that the longer he holds after the optimum period the worse becomes the ability to hold the pistol still. It takes two or three seconds for the muscles to adapt to the change in position from rest to the outstretched arm, and the period of good hold lasts for another eight seconds. If the shooter has trained well he will be able to hold longer but, at the same time, if the whole shoot lasts a long time he will become more fatigued in the end. He has to conserve his energy to last the whole shoot and beyond.

Concentration is really the key factor. The shooter has to remember all the points which go to make a good shot while he is taking in the deep breaths. As he lifts the pistol off the bench he must concentrate hard on getting the sight picture correct, with the foresight really sharp. Concentration is very energy-consuming and cannot be held for more than six seconds after reaching its peak. Some sources state that maximum concentration can only be held for three seconds.

When the factors are put together it can be shown that there is a short period when the peak of each factor coincides (see fig. 16). This is from about four and a half seconds from lift-off to a maximum of ten seconds, which gives five and a half seconds in which to fire the shot. This should be ample time.

The best time to fire will alter from shooter to shooter and also as conditions vary. If it is cold, it is important not to delay as the trigger finger will lose its sensitivity very quickly. Under such conditions it is worth sacrificing some degree of accuracy to get the shot away quickly, and the time can be as low as four seconds. The skill here is to build up the concentration *before* taking the aim and thus committing oneself to the shot at an early stage.

Concentration is necessary whenever there is hand–eye co-ordination and the better the concentration the better will be the result. One can think of other sports with similar sequences, such as golf. The golfer takes up his stance when addressing the ball and moves it until he considers the club will strike the ball in the right direction. He concentrates on the ball whilst smoothly swinging the club back and then releases the swing in a forward motion through the ball to its

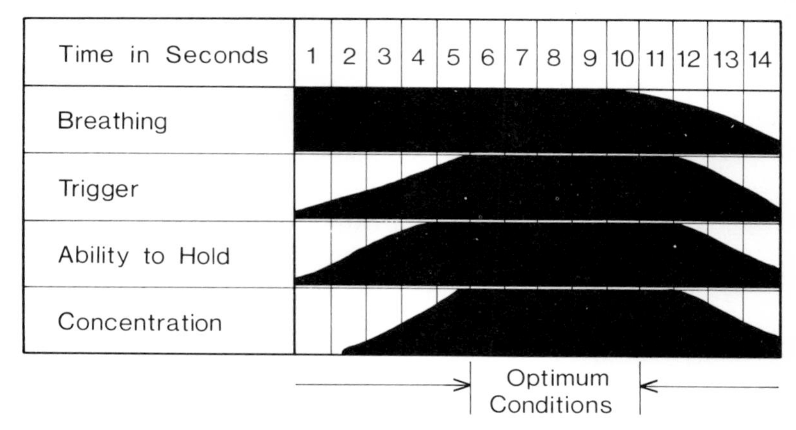

Fig. 16. *Diagram showing optimum shooting conditions*

natural follow-through. He will keep his head still until the follow-through is completed before looking to see where the ball has gone. During this time he will be in a cocoon of concentration and, even though as a top professional he may have a very large crowd watching him, he will not be disturbed until he has finished. If he is not quite satisfied with his shot he will often play the stroke again, to remind himself of his correct technique, and before he plays the shot he will have a practice swing or two. The batsman in cricket will concentrate on the bowler's delivery and endeavour to time his stroke to make a score. After playing the shot he will often repeat the shot and then relax before taking his guard or stance for the next ball.

The shooter must learn to develop this method of wrapping himself in his own cocoon of deep concentration, thinking about the next shot or series just before lifting the pistol from the bench and then funnelling that concentration from his eye to the tip of the foresight until his follow-through is completed. He can then see the result, analyse the reason for that result and prepare for his next shot.

There will be many an occasion in precision shooting when the shooter does not feel right when taking aim. Sometimes he will persist, hang on too long and release a poor shot. In timed shooting the shooter is committed once the targets are exposed. He has to judge as near as possible the moment when the targets will turn and build his concentration to that point, so that he is committed at that moment. The precision shooter can take his time, provided he completes within the time allotted, and can therefore abort the procedure if he does not feel ready. However, each time the pistol is raised energy is expended and therefore he should not lift too many times for each shot. I remember seeing a shooter raise his pistol eighteen times before he fired his first shot. Once he had fired that one the rest flowed easily and a good result was obtained. Such patience comes from knowing one's own technique and from determination not to fire until ready. The shooter must be in sufficient control of his actions to be able to take his finger off the trigger once he feels there is a doubt as any doubts will disturb the concentration.

The shooter will have to plan his shoot according to his own techniques, but he should always leave himself with adequate time to finish. Nothing is more disturbing than to realize that time is running out. It is no good having fired well initially and then having to rush the last few shots with a poor result. If training has been thorough, the shooter will have practised his timing and any anxiety about timing will be removed. The slow finisher is probably causing more anxiety to his fellow shooters and coach than to himself! Spare time should be built in to the shooter's timetable in case of any emergency, such as a minor fault to his pistol or the need to leave the range.

There are many variations in firing technique. Some shooters will put the pistol down after each shot, others will fire up to five shots without taking the hand from the grip. It is very difficult to stop a sequence of good shots but the shooter must recognize that in a long shoot he should give himself time to fully recover after each shot or series of shots. Once he has to question whether he should fire another shot before having a rest he must stop and rest or the thought of resting will intrude on his concentration.

Sometimes, in spite of all precautions a shoot will not be as good as one would hope. It is no good getting upset about it as this will only make matters worse. The positive action is to analyse each shot and to take positive steps to ensure that the next shot or series of shots is better. One's grouping capacity will give a potential for a score. One can have a shoot with all the shots around the circumference of the group giving a comparatively poor score. This is bad luck and not bad shooting. On the other hand it is no good getting elated when shooting above average halfway through a shoot. It is a sport of truths, and pride so easily comes before the fall. Each shot must be treated as a separate exercise; provided it falls within the shooter's own group it is satisfactory. After each shot or series of shots the shooter will record their position on his diagram to see that the group is a good shape and central. If it is off-centre the shooter must find the reason for this before making any sight changes. It may be that his stance or grip was not quite right. Normally the pistol will group in the same place and sight changes will be necessary only when external conditions change.

Having completed his shoot the shooter should wait until his neighbours have finished before packing up his equipment and walking off the range. When putting the gear away make sure the pistol is safe and has been given a wipe to remove any corrosive perspiration. If the shooter has finished early he should use the time to analyse the reason for this, to see whether it was to his advantage or not.

To summarize this chapter, the shooter should bear in mind that at all times the preparation must be thorough and that there is no room for second-best. The shooter must always try to do his best and not waste the whole effort of the shoot by one careless moment. He must prepare for each shot, fire each shot to the best of his ability, analyse each shot to determine how the best shots are fired and then relax between each shot.

6. Temperament

If the shooter has the will then, provided he can develop reliable techniques, his progress will depend upon the time and energy he can devote to training. Unfortunately, it will also depend on whether he has the necessary finance!

There have been many words written and said about the 'mental approach' to the major, or even the minor, occasion; the occasion being that shoot in new conditions which presents unknown factors. These might be the first match card, the first shoot on another range or the international match where the strength of the opposition is unknown. Animals fear the unknown. Man also has this fear but, because he is a rational creature, he can overcome his fear by training. The natural reaction to fear is an increase in the production of adrenalin. This acts on the heart, causing it to beat stronger and faster. When the danger is sensed adrenalin emphasizes awareness so that the body is ready to take immediate action and avoid the danger. The rate of breathing also quickens to provide the extra oxygen the increased blood flow demands. The increased heart and breathing rate will have a very deleterious effect on the shooting. The gun will not be steady and anxiety will cause such problems as trigger freeze.

Mental training, self-hypnosis and the use of alpha rhythms have all been put forward as ways in which the shooter can train himself to overcome match pressure. All shooters will, in the past, have experienced some such pressure, but I think that the shooter has the remedy in himself and, with the correct approach, the effects of such pressure can be avoided or much reduced.

The following analogy will throw some light on the matter. Most of us drive a car, some have limited experience and others have a great deal. Do any of us know when we meet another car how much experience the other driver has, unless he is showing certain symbols which indicate his prowess from the 'L' plate to the small badge, indistinguishable at a distance, of an Advanced Driver? We all know what to expect from the other driver in normal circumstances. The longer we drive, the greater our experience, and this experience enables us to drive with care and confidence. We do not know what to expect around the next bend, even if we know the road, nor if the car we are overtaking is going to swerve in front of us; but that does not prevent us from negotiating the bend or overtaking the car ahead. If we do meet an incident then there is a momentary injection of adrenalin while our brain rapidly scans all its previous experience and selects and acts upon a solution, i.e. experience takes over. In an extreme case the concentration will be so great that the experience is not recorded and there will be no memory of the action taken.

It is not difficult to relate this to shooting. While we are in the process of learning to shoot we do not have a badge to proclaim it, but our fellow shooters know our standard and we will not be entered for competitions at a level greater than our experience will tolerate. As more experience is gained then more challenges will be met.

The good driver is one who concentrates on his driving and enjoys a good technique and is always willing to consider changes to improve his technique. Similarly the shooter has to learn a good basic technique and constantly seek to improve it in the light of experience. He must apply himself wholly to the task in hand, avoiding external distraction and by deep concentration eliminate extraneous thoughts. He will then be able to withstand intrusion into his concentration with the knowledge that his technique will stand him in good stead under any circumstances.

There are two things that enable a person to achieve his own standard in most circumstances — skill and concentration.

The combination of these brings confidence. The object of shooting is to test oneself against a standard, albeit of one's own making. The target is the fixed object and the result of the test is the score on the target. The motivation is, firstly, the enjoyment of shooting itself and, secondly, to achieve recognition by improving one's standard. This means becoming more skilled, for the greater the skill the better the score.

Harris W. Johnson of the Municipal University of Omaha published in *Perceptual and Motor Skill*, 1961, a paper on 'Skill' which he defined as 'the ability to execute a pattern of behavioural elements in proper relation to a certain environment and this can be further stated as skill = speed × accuracy × form × adaptability.' Applying this to shooting, one can take each of the elements of skill and see how they affect the shooter. Here the instructor and/or coach should be involved as, although he can observe the results of his skill, the shooter will find it very difficult to examine by himself its differing elements.

The *speed* in which an operation is performed must have an important bearing on the result. If one is too hasty or too slow, or the timing is ragged it will upset all the effort put into the other elements. Speed in this context should also include all the preparatory time — getting to the range in plenty of time so that the preparations immediately before the shoot can be carried out calmly. Even have a little time in reserve in case of unforeseen events. (See Chapter 5 for the factors determining actual operation of the pistol at the optimum speed for each shooter.) The shooter in learning this element of skill will be advised by his instructor and coach.

Accuracy is not the result on the target but that required in performing the operation within the scope of the skill. In shooting, this will mean close attention to detail in the basics, i.e. stance, aim, grip and trigger, so that the pistol points in the right direction each and every time a shot is fired.

Form can be described as the co-ordination of the basic factors. As the separate principles are combined they will be adjusted one with another until the best combination is found.

Adaptability — this is really self-explanatory — means that in whatever circumstances the shooter finds himself he will be able to exercise his skill. There are people whose temperament makes it difficult for them to adapt and each will find his own limitations. Within their limitations they will find opportunities to exercise their skill and so obtain enjoyment and satisfaction from the sport.

There will, however, be a small group who can combine all the elements of skill and they will be the ones most likely to succeed at a higher level. The elements are not necessarily learned in the order stated. I think that the first should be accuracy, followed by form, then speed and, finally, adaptability. Each can be tested separately and together as the shooter progresses.

It is so easy for external factors to disturb the concentration. Even when wearing ear muffs, a conversation can intrude. There are no rules that prohibit all noise on a range, only some which request quiet. However, it is even easier for random thoughts to enter the mind than to be disturbed by outside noise. It is necessary to apply oneself in a positive manner to the shot by thinking one's way through all the details. Concentration is a positive factor and requires effort. The longer the shoot the harder it becomes. Many shooters have failed towards the end of a shoot because they knew it was near the end and subconsciously relaxed too early.

The other major cause of failure is the fear of failure. The desire to succeed becomes a desire not to fail and so a negative attitude comes into being. Instead of trying to shoot a good shot the shooter tries not to shoot a bad shot. This is, in my opinion, a lack of confidence in one's own ability and therefore a failure in training. If the shooter has the required degree of skill he knows what the result will be. It may be that there will be the occasional poor shot, but the end result should be roughly in line with his average. On some days it will be better and some days worse. It is no use worrying about the result of a shot before it is fired and not the slightest use afterwards! If the shooter trusts in his skill then he can have a positive approach and achieve his result with equanimity. If not he cannot forecast a result at all. This lack of trust in himself can be overcome by training, training and yet more training. The negative approach will only induce nervousness and an increase in adrenalin with the predicted poor result.

I do not believe that any form of hypnosis can make any real impact on the shooter's proficiency if the skill is not there. It is similar to an examination — if the lessons have not been learned there is no knowledge to answer the questions. No outside influences can provide a substitute for a missing or poor technique.

There has been much discussion on the subject of mental attitudes, perhaps with so much emphasis on the psychological side that the average shooter thinks that his attitude is one solution for his poor performances. If more emphasis were given to teaching the skills, so that the shooter knows his strength, it would not be necessary to find excuses for poor performances. Reasons can be given for poor performances not excuses. The reasons are capable of examination with a view to finding training programmes to eliminate them. This again would be positive thinking.

To summarize, therefore, to succeed, the shooter must learn the basic principles thoroughly, examine them in relation to his own particular needs, and constantly re-examine them to eliminate weaknesses, so that when the test takes place the foundation for success has been well laid.

7. Physical Training

The test of skills is the end result, i.e. what happens on the target. There are many classes of shooters: there are those who shoot for their own satisfaction without a care for the result, and there are others to whom success and improvement are the spur. I do not denigrate the 'fun' shooter. He has his place and is often the hard-working club member and, judging by the quantity of ammunition he sends up the range, a financial benefactor! He is getting out of the sport what he wants — enjoyment from his shooting and the social companionship of other shooters. Nevertheless, at some time, he may find that he is not getting satisfaction from his activities and he too will join in taking steps to improve his performance.

All shooters should have access to experience. It is hoped that in all clubs with pistol shooters there will be at least one qualified instructor or coach who will be able to teach the basic principles and lead the novice through a programme to a reasonable standard. Beyond that the shooter should still be able to call on experienced coaches. Coaching is in itself a skill, not only must the coach have the knowledge but he must also be able to instil confidence in his ability.

It will be necessary to cover training in such a manner that it will cater for the novice who has international aspirations. Progress will be gradual as one step must be consolidated before proceeding to the next. The way by which these steps are achieved is by training which is planned and arranged between the shooter and his instructor or coach.

Training falls into two main sections — physical and technical. It is no use trying to shoot successfully if unfit. It is just as important for the shooter to be fit as it is for the athlete. The shooter requires considerable stamina, as he has to produce the same effort at the end of a shoot as at the beginning if he is to maintain a reasonable standard throughout. He requires strength to keep a stable position, a good vascular and circulatory system to supply oxygen throughout his body and an efficient mechanism to remove waste products. He must also have a good sense of touch and good hand/eye co-ordination.

The ordinary active person is reasonably fit but the dedicated shooter will want a higher standard of fitness and will need to follow a proper programme. I think that the basic fitness programmes as shown in Dr Cooper's *Aerobics* (published by Bantam) will give the shooter his general fitness. Here the guiding principle is that monitored exertion will improve lung capacity and consequently improve blood circulation at a lower heart rate. The training involved is regular exertion with monitored recovery rate. When fit, the exertion will produce a faster heart beat to supply the body with oxygen-rich blood and to remove the waste products. When the exertion is over a fit person will resume his basic rate within a few minutes. A trained person can have a heart beat in the low 50s when at rest and this can rise into the 70s during exertion. At this rate it will be about the same as the average person at rest and will have no adverse effect on the ability to hold still. An untrained person will start with a pulse of 70 plus and when exerted this will rise to above 100. This will certainly be apparent when holding a pistol at arm's length.

One of the basic factors of a fit person is the relationship between height and weight. It is a feature of civilized society that a high proportion of the population is overweight. Too much weight throws stress on the heart, giving a high pulse at rest and consequently a too high rate when exercising. One of the first purposes of getting fit is to achieve a reasonable weight whilst not indulging in too severe a slimming programme. Slimming can be weakening, so a sensible approach must be made. It can be a wise step to consult one's doctor at this point. There are many systems of proper diet but, generally speaking, overeating puts on weight and undereating reduces it; but a minimum intake of solids and liquids is required to keep the body functioning. Looking at the top shooters, there are very few who look overweight and the majority are slim in relation to their height. Exercise by itself will not necessarily reduce weight — it will turn surplus fat into muscle and so weight could still be excessive. The programme should therefore be a combination of exercise and dieting. Fitness is not only a prerequisite of sport, it will have a useful work and social connotation, as a fit person is generally more alert.

The programme requires the same will and determination as applied to any objective where success is desired. A simple exercise programme may require up to two hours daily for six days a week. It is best done at the same time each day to make a good routine. Some prefer to exercise early in the morning and others prefer to wait until the day's work is done. In establishing a good routine an additional factor is introduced — that of discipline. To carry out the routine day in and day out (under any conditions) imposes a self-discipline which is a very good trait in other aspects of the sport. Often the training is carried out by the shooter on his own and he will be in a similar situation on the range.

General fitness is achieved by stamina-building, such as walking, running, swimming and cycling, and need not be fully suspended during the main period of competition. Even then, light exercises should be taken daily. Besides general fitness, exercises to develop the particular muscles concerned with pistol shooting should be carried out. The degree to which exercises are performed depends on each shooter. It is unnecessary and even harmful to over-exercise. Consideration of what is needed directs the shooter to the exercises needed. The body needs to be held erect and the pistol held at arm's length. The leg muscles should therefore be strong enough to support the abdomen and torso. General fitness training should be adequate for this purpose with some additional abdomen-muscle exercises. These can be press ups and back-lifting toe-touching work-outs. The shoulder and arm muscles are very important in holding the pistol and need strengthening to the point where the pistol can be held still at the end of a long shoot. Training should be repeated lifting of the required weight. The pistol itself can be used as the training aid and should be held at arm's length for up to a minute at a time. This should develop into an hour's exercise of, say, one minute up and two minutes down. By using the pistol, the correct muscles are involved and the pistol is held by the proper grip (but it is not necessary to aim).

The forearm and wrists can be developed either by wrist exercisers or by winding up a weight on a broomstick. The former are twist grips with an adjustable friction so that they can be set for any desired torque. With the latter simple device, the stick can first be held close to the body with a minimum weight, and wound up and unwound a minimum number of times. As time goes on the distance from the body, the weight and the number of times can be gradually increased. Exercise should continue until the arms feel tired and the time involved will increase as the muscles strengthen. Fingers and hands can be exercised quite simply by holding and squeezing a rubber ball. The ball should be held tightly until the muscles indicate they have had enough exertion, then relax for a couple of minutes and squeeze the ball again and so on. Another exercise is to stretch the whole hand to the finger tips slowly and then, after holding the hand stretched for a short period, make a fist, keeping the tension in the muscles. This should be repeated for, say, five times, then rest before trying again. Such exercises can be done anywhere or at any time and do not need any special equipment.

If the shooter is new to exercise then he will certainly feel the effects to begin with. If Dr Cooper's book is followed, a gradual increase in exertion will not be too arduous. If you intend to follow a programme seriously it might be worthwhile having a medical check-up first. It is doubtful whether any immediate improvement will be noticed in shooting performance. On the contrary, by developing unused muscles shooting might temporarily suffer, but improvement will follow. In the long term, improvement in fitness must have a beneficial effect not only in shooting, but in general well-being. There will be times when training will not be possible and between seasons it will not be necessary. When restarting, the build-up must be gradual to avoid any strain. If at any time there is strain, training should avoid that area of exercise and, if rest does not help, medical advice should be sought.

8. Technical Training

The training for physical fitness and better technique go hand in hand. Both are the means to the end and until the end is reached, the emphasis is on training. In my opinion, for serious shooters there are only three types of shooting; training, sighting and match. I do not like 'practice' shooting and think that 'training' shooting gives more point to the effort made. Every shot must be fired for a purpose — ammunition is too expensive to waste. As I have said before, the fun shooter shoots as he likes and if he keeps to the rules, especially safety, he has his place in the sport.

Technical training begins away from the range. On the assumption that there is an interval between shooting seasons, training will start about a couple of months before the season opens. In many cases, however, the season is continuous, for different disciplines cover different periods and many shooters shoot more than one discipline. At the close of the season in question the pistols must have a thorough clean and probably a check over by a competent armourer to ensure that they are put away in perfect condition.

The shooter has to train himself to the pitch of perfection which allows him to start the season at about where he previously left off. He should study his shooting pattern during the interval to see where his weak points lie and so arrange his training to take these into account.

Having had a rest, the muscles and the hand/eye co-ordination will have lost their fine tuning and it will be necessary to retune them. One can visualize a rough programme to achieve this. In week one and two you will need to spend fifteen to thirty minutes daily on stance and grip. The shooter will take up his stance and then pick up the pistol, not forgetting to check for safety, and point it in the general direction of the aiming mark. No attempt should be made to aim or to release the trigger. Hold the pistol up for about twenty seconds and gradually, by the end of the second week, increase this to two minutes. The pistol should be held up only until the muscles of the arm feel that they are beginning to get tired. Holding beyond this point has little value. It may be that when the pistol is first gripped after the lay-off, the grip does not feel right. Examine this critically to determine whether it is the rest that has allowed the hand to lose the feel of the grip or whether during the previous season the grip was not quite right. This should be apparent from a critical examination of shooting records. If the grip needs alteration now is the time to do it.

The next stage is to include trigger release. The method is to continue as above but to concentrate on releasing the trigger correctly. All this training will be dry firing. It does not matter at this stage if the trigger is released too early or too slowly, as long as it is released using the correct technique. This period will cover another fortnight, by the end of which training should occupy an hour a day. The time spent will vary according to which discipline is being exercised but if the full hour is not being used then the concentration must be greater. The rapid-fire shooter will start his training with the raise for the first shot to ensure accuracy, and timing will follow.

The final stage will be to incorporate aiming into the sequence and then to co-ordinate all the functions to ensure that a shot is fired when the shooter decides it should be fired. Only then will it be necessary to 'live' fire to put the edge on this training. Returning to the range for live firing the shooter must use the time to the best advantage. It may be that, as a result of the examination of the previous season's shooting, a change of technique is desirable. This will have been practised in the dry firing period. It is very difficult to change an established technique and quite a long period of training is necessary to prove or disprove the benefit of a change. It is therefore important that the new technique must not be coloured by knowledge of the previous one as, initially, there may not be any apparent improvement.

It will not be necessary at the beginning of this training period to fire much ammunition — quality is more important than quantity. When the techniques have been established the training can and should be extended and will include shoots longer than the match course. Again it is important that each shot or each string is fired with concentration and determination, as in a match, otherwise no value is gained. The experience so gained in training is then drawn upon when the match occurs, and the experience in the match is consequently used in training.

Various training schedules have been produced and the shooter should be advised by his coach which is best for his needs. I will however describe some methods, the first of which is 'Calling the Shot'. This can be used in all forms of pistol shooting. A sheet of paper or card is inscribed with a series of crosses, enough to cover a training period. The lines of the cross represent the vertical and horizontal axis of the target, rings can be imposed to represent the shot value but do not need to be in proportion. The shooter fires a few sighting shots to remind himself of his technique and accustom himself to the conditions. He then passes his telescope to an assistant and fires a shot. After the follow-through he 'calls the shot', i.e. he tells the assistant where he considers the shot to have gone. He may call 'good shot, probably a 9 at 12'. The assistant plots this on one of the crosses and then spots the shot, recording its position and value (see fig. 17). This continues for a number of shots, perhaps in series of ten. The 'called' shots are then compared with the actual strikes. It is an exercise in concentration and can show up faults. The shooter must be honest and declare the shot as he sees it, not as he might have hoped. If he has a doubt it is better to declare the poorer image rather than the aspired one. He will also state if the shot was badly released or poorly aimed. If there is a

Example of record to be completed

Call	+	+	+	+	+	+
Shot	+	+	+	+	+	+

Examples of completing the record

	A			B		
Call						
	10 at 10	9 at 12	10 at 2	10 central	9 low	10 high
Shot						
	10 at 8	10 central	9 at 4	8	9	9

Fig. 17. *Shot calling*

Comment:

A: All called high but all shots about 2 inches below call. If shots had been called central the strikes would all be low—if this pattern continues sights need to be raised.

B: Shooter not definite enough in call. More training needed in this exercise. Discrepancy probably due to inconsistency in concentrating on sight picture.

discrepancy between the shots called and the strike an explanation must be found. The shooter will have concentrated on his technique because he is determined to give of his best. By making a declaration each time, he is shooting one shot at a time and only concerned with that one shot. By having to concentrate to recognize the sight picture at the time of trigger release, he is improving his recognition of the correct sight picture. He can carry out this exercise by himself but must declare and record his shot, writing with his non-shooting hand or putting down his pistol, *before* looking through the telescope. Even in a match the shooter can make such a record. Although this primarily applies to precision shooting it can also apply to rapid fire as this shooter can remember his point of aim for each target and can call his shots in strings of five.

Another method of shooting training is to plot a series of shots so that the whole shoot can be recorded on one plot. Divide the plot into vertical and horizontal axes through the centre of the target and count the number of shots in each quadrant. If they are equally distributed there is little at fault and it shows that the sights are correctly zeroed. If, however, there are more shots in one quadrant than another, a reason (not an excuse) must be found for the discrepancy. For example, if there are more shots in the upper quadrants, equally distributed from side to side, it is likely that the sights need lowering. A series of diagrams will best illustrate these points (see fig. 18).

By plotting the shots irrespective of the score the shooter will be able to watch his group without thinking of the score. If he is watching his score and is getting tens and nines he will probably think he is doing well, but an overall examination of the group could indicate a small shift would have given him a couple of more points, i.e. 94 instead of 92. The shooter must always remember he is shooting a group, and the smaller the group with its mean point of impact on the centre of the target, the higher will be the score. Any odd shots outside the group will be apparent at the time of release if the shooter is concentrating on his proper techniques.

Earlier mention was made of shooting on a blank card. This is not only a method of training a novice but should be a frequent exercise for all shooters. It reminds them of their

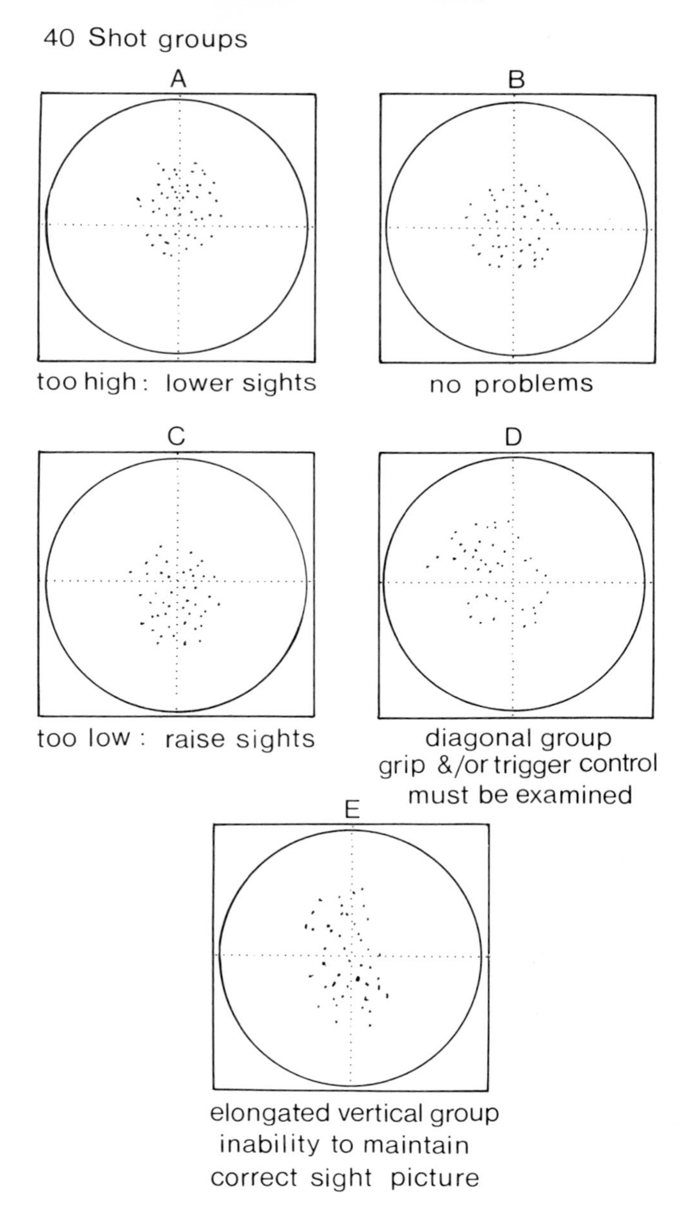

Fig. 18. *Fault finding: each plot shows a whole shoot*

techniques and can show up faults. It has been said that the good shots do not matter but the bad ones do. For example, the shooter shoots a card, say ten shots, but before he sees the card the centre is cut out, how much is cut out depending on the skill of the shooter. By this means shots which were skilful are discarded and the shooter has to account for those which still show on the card.

Another useful method, known as step shooting, can be competitive. It may be carried out by shooters of any level, as the steps are adjusted to the shooter. Each shooter has six chances in which to complete five steps. Before he starts he must have sufficient skill to be able to declare an average. Assuming the shooter has an average of 82, he will fire ten shots and have to score 82 or over. If he succeeds, he will go to step two, if not, he has to repeat step one, but will then have no second chance on any subsequent step. If he fails he starts again. Having succeeded with his first ten shots he fires five for a score of 41; the third step will be three shots for 25 (i.e. the proportion of three-tenths of 82 rounded up); fourth step will be two shots for 17 and the final step one shot for an 8. The fewer steps left the harder it becomes because there is no room for recovery. For instance in stage four, if the first shot is a 7, the shooter must get a 10 for the second shot. This can be frustrating but enjoyable!

There are, no doubt, other exercises designed to improve the shooter's technique and his skills, by reducing the size of the group. All shooters have an average and should work to improve it. Generally the graph of improvement is not a smooth curve or a straight line but has steps and plateaux. In the period just before taking a step forward the score will fluctuate and, having taken the step, there is a period of consolidation before the next noticeable improvement. The serious shooter will recognize these features and work hard towards the next step.

9. Fault Finding

If the correct basic techniques have been thoroughly learned there should be few faults. However, errors in technique *will* be made and the evidence will be on the target. This should always be examined critically and, if possible, discussed with the instructor or coach. It is best to do this at the time, when the events are fresh in the mind.

The evidence will be a misplaced group or shots outside the group. One must assume that the pistol has been correctly zeroed and the sights adjusted accordingly. The shooter may have called a series of shots that would predict the pattern on the target and would then know what he has to do to rectify the error. It is the shots (or pattern of shots) for which there is no immediate answer that will be harder to analyse and correct as it is easier to offer an excuse than to look for a reason. The shooter can sometimes become too complacent about his capabilities and not take proper care over the details of his technique.

If the coach or instructor is present during the shooting he can observe the actions of the shooter. To be of any value such observation must be detailed, as a general examination of the shooter is unlikely to find a fault in technique. The coach must look at a particular point, such as how the pistol is being picked up or whether the finger always falls on the trigger in the same place. It may take some time before such detailed observation produces results, as each observation has to be compared with the evidence on the target. This may be helped by following the plotting procedure described in Chapter 8, with additional advice from the coach.

The displaced group can be due to incorrect sight adjustment, especially if it is displaced in one direction (i.e. too high or too low) but within the capability of the shooter. If the group does, however, shift from shoot to shoot or from target to target then it can be due to either an inconsistent point of aim or a variation in grip. A critical examination of technique and attention to detail should resolve these problems.

If the group takes on a diagonal picture the fault will probably be due to faulty trigger control. This can also be due to a change in grip from shot to shot and, therefore, a change in location of the trigger finger or a fluctuating control of the trigger. (Faults caused by aiming errors have been fully explained in Chapter 4 and no further comment is needed here.)

There is another reason for displaced shots, particularly in the case of an experienced shooter. He will know whether he is shooting within his capability and should be able to call each shot to within an inch. If misplaced shots are appearing on the target for no logical reason (from the point of view of technique) another cause must be sought. If a couple of random shots appear the pistol must be examined. First, a check should be made on the sights; it is not unknown for sights to fall off in the middle of a shoot and a loose sight will produce a haphazard result on the target. Secondly, the trigger should be tested by dry firing a number of releases. The shooter will know if it is functioning properly; if not it must be stripped and repaired. It could also be due to grips that have come slightly loose. Before resuming the course of fire it is wise to check the barrel. Even a good barrel will sometimes pick up a little lead and the bullet will not follow a predicted flight. The barrel will have to be cleaned before examination (this only takes a few minutes) and even cleaning it thoroughly to remove any lead can be done on the range.

If a pistol is at fault the range officer should be informed in case longer time is needed to repair the fault. The rules do allow repair of weapons and even substitution, if the original cannot be repaired within a reasonable time. In precision shooting there is usually enough time to make minor repairs or adjustments within the time allowed, but in rapid and timed fire the dispensation of the range officer must be sought. One must remember that the rules do not allow any scoring concessions for a badly maintained pistol or for a malfunction within the control of the shooter. An experienced confident shooter should immediately recognize an error due to the pistol and take the necessary steps to rectify the fault.

Very few faults are caused by poor ammunition. The manufacturers, in a very competitive market, try to ensure through quality control that their products keep a high standard. There will be the occasional misfire, but before blaming the ammunition make sure that the rim of the cartridge has been correctly struck by the firing pin. Sometimes after a series of shots grease builds up on the face of the block so the pin does not travel far enough to strike the rim properly. Also, if grease accumulates around the firing pin it can force the pin too far out or too far in again causing a malfunction. Do not persevere with the struck round, in case it *is* faulty, but fire another after inspecting the pistol. When the shoot has finished, the suspect cartridge should be tested, loaded so that the pin strikes a different part of the rim. If it does not fire, take a note of the batch number and refer the cartridge to the ammunition manufacturer at the earliest opportunity. They usually have a representative at the more important meetings. If at the shooting club then feed the information back through the club secretary. The manufacturers are quite keen to have batches of faulty ammunition returned, as it enables them to check on their quality controls.

It is doubtful if there will ever be a perfect shooter, some will be better than others and there will always be room for improvement at every level. The pistol and the ammunition will always be able to group better than the shooter holding the pistol. Techniques can improve through training, which may bring to light faults which by critical analysis, whether by the shooter himself or in conjunction with his instructor or coach, can be eradicated. It should never be forgotten that shooting is a sport. The more the shooter puts into his sport the more he will get out of it, whether as a competitor or an official.